Scratch 1.4

Beginner's Guide

Learn to program while creating interactive stories, games, and multimedia projects using Scratch

Michael Badger

[PACKT] PUBLISHING

BIRMINGHAM - MUMBAI

Scratch 1.4
Beginner's Guide

First published: July 2009

Production Reference: 1060709

Published by Packt Publishing Ltd.
32 Lincoln Road
Olton
Birmingham, B27 6PA, UK.

ISBN 978-1-847196-76-7

www.packtpub.com

Cover Image by Vinayak Chittar (vinayak.chittar@gmail.com)

Credits

Author

Michael Badger

Reviewer

Tom McKearney

Acquisition Editor

David Barnes

Development Editor

Dhiraj Chandiramani

Technical Editor

Abhinav Prasoon

Indexer

Rekha Nair

Editorial Team Leader

Gagandeep Singh

Project Team Leader

Lata Basantani

Project Coordinator

Joel Goveya

Proofreader

Jade Schuler

Production Coordinator

Shantanu Zagade

Cover Work

Shantanu Zagade

About the Author

Michael Badger is a technical communicator with a history of helping others use their computer software and technology. For fun, Michael reads computer books and blogs about technology. When he finally decides to disconnect, he spends his spare time fishing, growing pigs, raising honeybees, and tending the family.

Michael also wrote Zenoss Core Network and System Monitoring, a step-by-step guide to configuring, using, and adapting the free Open Source network monitoring system.

Share your feedback about this book at http://www.scratchguide.com.

Writers work hours at a time in isolation, but bringing a book from concept to finished product requires the support of many people. My support starts at home with my wife Christie's encouragement and my son Cameron's early bedtime. Cameron, when you're old enough to read, we'll create some games together.

Early in this project, I received thoughtful, timely, and sensible feedback from my editor David Barnes. Thanks for the great advice.

I thank the reviewer, who took time to read and respond critically to my work for which I will be forever grateful. Know that I appreciate every correction, suggestion, and improvement he offered. This book benefits from his attention.

About the Reviewer

Tom McKearney has been doing custom software development for 16 years on projects ranging from Automated Weather Observation, Vehicle Management Systems, Biometric Identification, Battle Simulations, and various financial applications. He is a self-described "geek" whose hobbies include tinkering with random electronics parts, beer brewing and reading excessively. Tom lives in the suburbs of Baltimore, Maryland, and currently specializes in Microsoft's .NET technologies while working for Applied Information Sciences (www.appliedis.com) in Reston, Virginia, U.S.

He was previously a technical reviewer of *"Quality Web Systems: Performance, Security, and Usability," Addison-Wesley Professional (September 2, 2001), 0201719363* written by Elfriede Dustin, Jeff Rashka, and Douglas McDiarmid.

Go to http://www.pearsonhighered.com/educator/academic/product/ 0,3110,0201719363,00.html for more information about this book.

Table of Contents

Preface

When we program, we solve problems. In order to solve problems, we think, take action, and reflect upon our efforts. Scratch teaches us to program using a fun, accessible environment that's as easy as dragging and dropping blocks from one part of the screen to another.

In this book, we will program games, stories, and animations using hands-on examples that get us thinking and tinkering. For each project, we start with a series of steps to build something. Then, we pause to put our actions into context so that we can relate our code to the actions on Scratch's stage. Throughout each chapter, you'll encounter challenges that encourage you to experiment and learn.

As you begin working through the examples in the book, you won't be able to stop your imagination, and the ideas will stream as fast as you can think of them. Write them down. You'll quickly realize there are a lot of young minds in your home, classroom, or community group that could benefit from Scratch's friendly face. Teach them, please.

What this book covers

Chapter 1 provides an overview of Scratch, its features, and how it can help you teach 21st century learning skills to your children and students.

Chapter 2 guides us through the installation of Scratch on Windows, OS X, and Linux. This chapter also helps you run the Scratch programming environment from a USB flash drive.

Chapter 3 explores the Scratch interface and allows us to create some simple scripts that demonstrate how easily we can build a project. This is a high-speed tour of Scratch that gets us tinkering and thinking about what's possible.

Chapter 4 teaches us how to create an animated birthday card and a slideshow of our favorite photos.

Chapter 5 allows us to horse around as we develop a barnyard humor book that lets us narrate multiple scenes. There's no need to hold the applause.

Chapter 6 takes a classic pong game and gives it a little personality by adding a troll, switching levels, and keeping score.

Chapter 7 takes us to the fortune-teller, but before we learn the random answers to all our deepest questions, we must create our game using the Magic 8 ball's fortunes.

Chapter 8 uses mathematical formulas and graphs to help us answer the question, "Would you rather have a dollar that doubles every day or a lump sum of money?" The answer may surprise you.

Chapter 9 explains how to share your project with the Scratch community and how to promote it to you friends and fans.

Chapter 10 shows us how to connect a webcam and an external sensor board to our computer and delivers real-world stimuli as input to Scratch projects.

What you need for this book

All you need is an imagination and a willingness to experiment. You will also need a computer with Scratch 1.4 installed. Most modern computers should easily run the latest version of Scratch; however, the Scratch team makes Scratch 1.2.1 available on the Scratch Download page for older systems. Here are the system requirements as defined by the Scratch team:

Display: 1024 x 768
        16-bit color or higher

Disk Space: At least 120 MB

Operating Systems:

- Windows 2000 or higher for Scratch 1.3
- Windows 98 users can use Scratch 1.2.1
- Mac OS X 10.4 for Scratch 1.3
- Mac OS X 10.3 for Scratch 1.2.1
- Linux support via WINE
- Native Linux support is experimental

If you want to take advantage of Scratch's audio and recording features, you will need a sound card, speakers, and a microphone.

Who this book is for

Scratch is a teaching language, so it's ideal for people who want to learn how to program or teach others how to program. Educators and parents will learn how to program using Scratch, and they can use Scratch to teach 21st century learning skills to their students and children.

The 21st century learning skills help develop digital literacy by teaching children how to design, think critically, collaborate, communicate, and program in a computer language.

No previous computer programming knowledge is required. If you know how to send email, create documents, or create presentations, then you have the prerequisite skills to learn how to program in Scratch.

For beginning programmers, this book will teach the basic concepts that you can then utilize to learn more advanced languages, such as Ruby, PHP, and Python.

Parents, are you stuck with a child who wants to play video games all night? Make a new rule. Your child can play a video game only if he or she programs the game first.

Conventions

In this book, you will find a number of styles of text that distinguish between different kinds of information. Here are some examples of these styles, along with an explanation of their meaning:

Code words in text are shown as follows: "We can include other contexts through the use of the `include` directive."

New terms and **important words** are shown in bold. Words that you see on the screen, in menus or dialog boxes for example, appear in our text like this: "Clicking the **Next** button moves you to the next screen."

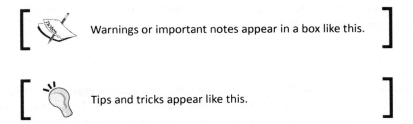

Warnings or important notes appear in a box like this.

Tips and tricks appear like this.

Reader feedback

Feedback from our readers is always welcome. Let us know what you think about this book—what you liked or disliked. Reader feedback is important for us to develop titles that you really get the most out of.

To send us general feedback, simply drop an email to feedback@packtpub.com, and mention the book title in the subject of your message.

If there is a book that you need and would like to see us publish, please send us a note in the **SUGGEST A TITLE** form on www.packtpub.com or email suggest@packtpub.com.

If there is a topic in which you have expertise and you are interested in either writing or contributing to a book, please see our author guide on www.packtpub.com/authors.

Customer support

Now that you are the proud owner of a Packt book, we have a number of things to help you to get the most from your purchase.

Downloading the example code for the book

Visit http://www.packtpub.com/files/code/6767_Code.zip to directly download the example code.

The downloadable files contain instructions on how to use them.

Errata

Although we have taken every care to ensure the accuracy of our contents, mistakes do happen. If you find a mistake in one of our books—maybe a mistake in text or code—we would be grateful if you would report this to us. By doing so, you can save other readers from frustration, and help us to improve subsequent versions of this book. If you find any errata, please report them by visiting http://www.packtpub.com/support, selecting your book, clicking on the **let us know** link, and entering the details of your errata. Once your errata are verified, your submission will be accepted and the errata added to any list of existing errata. Any existing errata can be viewed by selecting your title from http://www.packtpub.com/support.

Piracy

Piracy of copyright material on the Internet is an ongoing problem across all media. At Packt, we take the protection of our copyright and licenses very seriously. If you come across any illegal copies of our works in any form on the Internet, please provide us with the location address or web site name immediately so that we can pursue a remedy.

Please contact us at copyright@packtpub.com with a link to the suspected pirated material.

We appreciate your help in protecting our authors and our ability to bring you valuable content.

Questions

You can contact us at questions@packtpub.com if you are having a problem with any aspect of the book, and we will do our best to address it.

1
Welcome to Scratch!

Learn how to create animations, interactive stories, and games the drag-and-drop way using the computer programming language **Scratch**. *Scratch provides an intuitive interface that makes learning to program fun, easy, and well-suited as an educational tool for our children and students.*

We don't need to artificially restrict Scratch to the classroom though it makes a fantastic teaching tool. Anyone with a desire to learn a programming language can use Scratch as an introductory language. Perhaps you've tried other languages, such as Ruby, PHP, Java, or Python and had trouble getting started for one reason or another. Even if you can barely create a presentation using PowerPoint or OpenOffice.org, you'll find comfort in Scratch's building-block approach to programming.

After using Scratch, programming will make sense. It will seem easy. It will bring a smile to your face.

Whether you want to improve your digital literacy skills by learning to program or you want to learn a new tool to help you teach your students, here's to happy Scratchin'.

What is Scratch?

Scratch is developed by the Lifelong Kindergarten group at the MIT Media Lab. See http://scratch.mit.edu for more information. The Lifelong Kindergarten group at the MIT Media Lab developed Scratch as a teaching language specifically for 8 to 16 year olds, but there's nothing stopping the rest of us from enjoying the Scratch experience and sharpening our 21st century learning skills.

21st century learning skills

Learning: We do it for life. We should help our children develop skills that will help them keep learning in an increasingly digital environment.

Using Scratch, we learn how to design, think, collaborate, communicate, analyze, and program in a computer language. Many of these ideas incorporate 21st century learning skills. If you'd like more information about 21st century learning skills, visit the Partnership for 21st Century Skills web site at `http://www.21stcenturyskills.org`.

By the time we make our cat dance for the first time, we'll forget all about the academic research and theories behind Scratch. Instead, we'll be focused on discovering the next idea.

How to use Scratch?

I couldn't begin to suggest every possible way for you to use Scratch; that's why we have an imagination. However, here are a few ideas to get you started.

Use Scratch to teach yourself or your students how to program. That's the obvious one.

Use Scratch to demonstrate math concepts. For example, when it's time to teach variables, set up an interactive game that uses a variable to keep score or moves based on the variable data. Scratch can also demonstrate the X and Y coordinate system.

Inspire your kids to read and write. Find a story and animate each scene, or encourage them to animate the story. Turn their persuasive essays into a Scratch project.

Have a child who only wants to play video games? Make a deal. Your child can play only the games he or she creates with Scratch.

I'm sure you've got a lot of ideas flowing in your mind by now. Keep writing them down no matter how hard, easy, obvious, or silly they seem to be. The next one might be your best idea yet.

Programming concepts

With Scratch, we'll learn how to turn our imaginations into games, stories, and animations, and in the process, we'll learn some common programming concepts. If you're already a knowledgeable programmer, then you'll find out what Scratch has to offer your students.

The Scratch team publishes several resources to help educators, including a Programming Concepts guide, which I've summarized below:

Concept	Description
Program Design	When we design a program, we turn our imagination into something that can be shared with others. We create the flow of the program, the interface, and the actions each sprite takes to tell our story.
Loops (Iteration)	Loops iterate through a series of steps for as long as we tell the program to run the loop. We can use other programming concepts, such as conditional statements, to control the loop.
Conditional Statements	Check to see if a statement is true. For example, **if 4 > 0** is a conditional statement.
Boolean Logic	Boolean logic operators include **and**, **or**, and **not**. **If 4 > 0 and 4 > 1** is one example.
Variables	Variables store text or numbers for reuse in the program. They come in global and local types. For example, **if x > 0** creates a conditional statement where x is 0, 1, 2, or anything else we define.
Arrays (Lists)	Arrays are similar to variables in that they store dynamic data. However, a list stores multiple values in the same way a grocery list stores a group of items.
Events	An action in the program prompts another part of the program to take an action. For example, when the Space bar is pressed, the sprite hides.
Synchronization and Coordination	Programming a sprite to receive a broadcast message from another sprite coordinates a cause and effect. Broadcasting a message and waiting for all the other sprites to act on the broadcast synchronizes the action.
Threads	Creating two scripts to run on the same control enables parallel execution. For example, programming four different sprites to pixelate when the flag (green in color) is clicked creates four threads.
Dynamic Interaction	Dynamic interaction provides real-time input into the Scratch program in order to manipulate the sprite in some way. For example, the position of the mouse is always known, so we can create a sprite that always follows the mouse position.
Random Numbers	Random numbers are picked from the range we specify.

Programming limitations

As of Scratch version 1.4, there are a few limitations with the language. As taken from Scratch's Programming Concepts guide, here are the concepts Scratch does not cover: functions, recursion, exception handling, file input/output, inheritance, parameter and return values, and defining classes of objects.

If that last paragraph sounds like gibberish, don't worry about it.

Scratch anatomy

For those of us with a desire to use geek terms, Scratch provides an **Integrated Development Environment (IDE)** that enables us to design, program, and run our projects. Don't worry; we'll just call it the Scratch interface from this point forward. You can see it in the following screenshot:

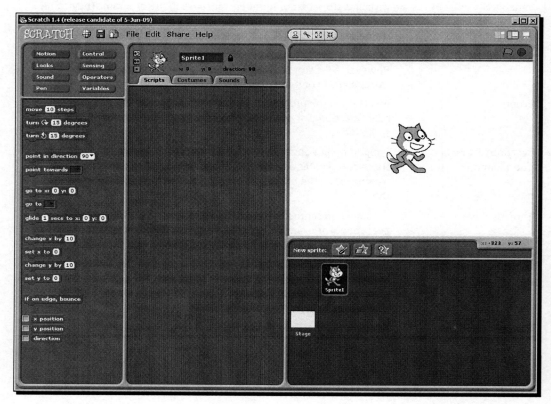

In the following chapters, we will become familiar with the parts of the Scratch interface, so we don't need to spend a lot of time reviewing what each button does. Let's instead stick with the big concepts.

Building blocks

If we review the Scratch interface from left to right, everything we need to create a project is readily accessible. To the left side of the interface, we have categories of blocks that are grouped by the kinds of tasks they perform. They are **Motion**, **Looks**, **Sound**, **Pen**, **Control**, **Sensing**, **Operators**, and **Variables**.

Throughout the book, I'll refer to these categories of blocks as **palettes**.

The palette of blocks available to us as Scratch programmers are analogous to the palette of colors an artist mixes when creating a painting. Each type of block is color-coded so that we can easily identify them in our scripts.

Write the script

When we create our Scratch programs, we build a group of scripts that tell our story. Instead of using words as you're used to reading them on this page, we'll build our scripts from the palette of blocks.

We'll drag, drop, and snap them into place in the **Scripts** area to create our story. The following screenshot shows a script that was taken from one of the sample projects included with Scratch:

If we read the blocks shown in the screenshot from top to bottom, we should have a good idea of the story this sprite tells. Who doesn't love a knock-knock joke?

To see our story play out, we watch the stage.

Watch the story

When it comes time to review the script, we watch it on the stage. It's here that we get to see our ideas turn into reality.

And just like the stage at the theater, we can see from our screenshot that we can have a cast of characters to entertain us.

Scratch even provides a built-in image editor to help us create and modify our characters, which we call **sprites**.

Built-in image editor

Scratch includes a simple image editing environment called the **Paint Editor** that allows us to apply text, color, and shape to our sprites and backgrounds.

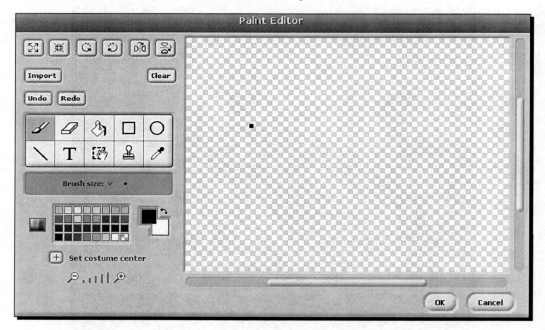

The Paint Editor allows us to do the following:

- Create shapes and text
- Import and edit images
- Apply color treatments
- Resize, rotate, and flip an image

The Paint Editor is available from multiple points within the Scratch interface, as we'll see later in the book.

Interface promotes tinkering

The structure of the Scratch interface makes it easy for us to tinker and explore ideas. As we create, we evaluate our work and determine if the results meet our expectations. It's very easy because everything happens in one interface.

We don't have to compile code, switch windows, upload files to a server, or encounter any number of obstacles to see if our code works. Scratch enables us to modify the program as it runs and see the results in real time.

Learning Scratch

I took a project-based approach in this book. So, instead of working with a single project, each chapter creates something new.

While I may want to tell a story, you may want to create a game, build an animation, or explore an interactive art project. By working with a range of projects, we'll quickly learn and focus on the concepts that matter the most.

The more ideas we generate, the better off we'll be when it comes to helping our children or students learn Scratch. Feel free to adapt the projects in this book to your own needs. Reuse them as needed.

It's true that Scratch will teach us how to program, but it really just provides us a visual framework. We can use this framework to express creative thinking while we learn how to do the following:

◆ Design the project's scenes and interfaces

◆ Analyze behavior and troubleshoot problems

◆ Improve the project through revisions

◆ Share our imagination with our peers through our projects

I expect that after we get started, you'll have your own ideas about a project or a variation on the current exercise. Keep a pen nearby and write those ideas in the margin.

Here's a chapter-by-chapter look at what we'll cover in the book.

Welcome to Scratch!

You're reading this chapter right now. You'll find out what we can expect from Scratch and how it can help us teach 21st century learning skills.

Installation

Scratch is a cross-platform application, which means you can use it on Windows, Macintosh, and Linux operating systems. In this chapter, we'll look at the installation procedure on each operating system and even learn how to run Scratch from your USB flash drive.

We'll also make sure your web browser can view Java applets, which is the technology Scratch uses to publish projects on the Web.

Start Scratching

We will explore the Scratch interface and create some simple scripts that demonstrate how easily we can build a project. This is a high-speed tour of Scratch that gets us tinkering and thinking about what's possible.

Sharing is a central philosophy to Scratch. Each project we upload to the community web site will be available under a Creative Commons Attribution-Share Alike license. Since we don't have any work to share, this gives us an idea of where we're heading. We'll demonstrate how to find and download a project to inspire us.

Graphics and Slideshows

In Chapter 4, we will slow down the pace and talk about the concepts in more detail. We will also create two projects; the first will be an animated birthday card, and the second will be a picture slideshow using our favorite photos.

We'll use the Paint Editor to design images for the project and transform those images with various graphic effects. We'll also learn how to control the sequence of our scenes.

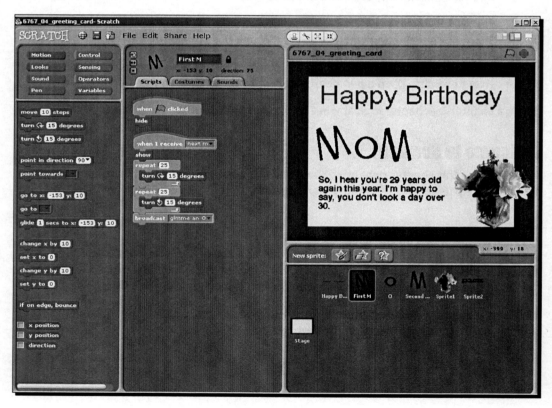

Storytelling

We will develop a barnyard humor book that lets us shine as storytellers. We'll find out how to turn our chapters into scenes using Scratch.

Our sprites will change appearances, speak, make noise, and report to specific stage coordinates. The emphasis will be on how to use these elements to tell their story.

Arcade Games

In Chapter 6, we will take a classic pong game that's included with Scratch and give it a little personality. Our Scratch installation comes with a classic looking pong game, so rather than start over, we'll modify it.

The central concepts in this chapter include dynamic interaction and conditional statements to control how our paddle and ball move across the stage. We will also introduce variables as a way to store and retrieve information for use in our programs.

Games of Fortune

Here, we will visit the fortune-teller and learn the answers to all our deepest questions. It might be more appropriate to say we'll build the fortune-teller game, so we shouldn't really trust our "fortunes."

In Chapter 7, we will combine what we know about variables with lists, also known as **arrays**. We will use the lists to store information about our fortunes and use random numbers to retrieve the data. Variables store dynamic data that we use to determine how our program should behave.

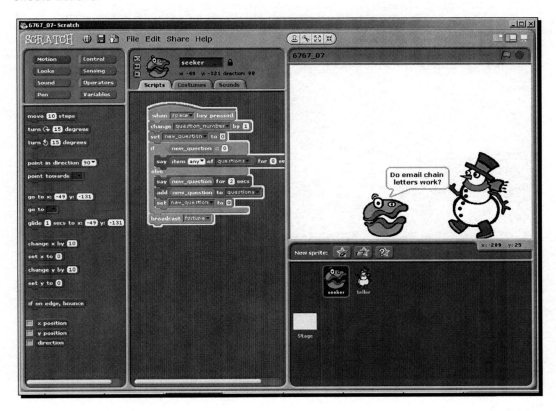

Math and Finance

Chapter 8 proposes the following problem: Would you rather have a dollar today that doubles every day for a set number of days? Or, would you rather have a lump sum of money? We will build the program to answer that question.

This chapter compares the power of doubling versus the accrual of simple interest. We'll make the math problem interactive and allow the user to input custom starting values. Then, we'll show the results in a graphical format using the pen tool.

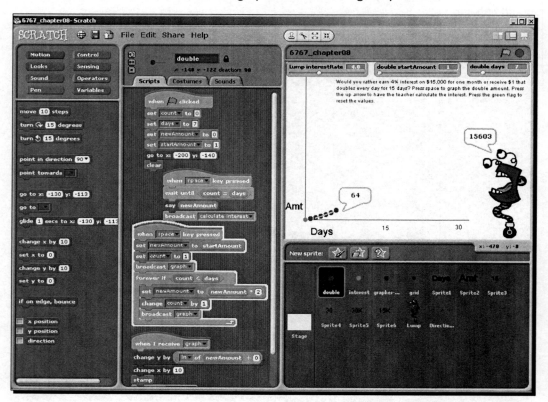

Share!

We're back to sharing. In Chapter 3, we learned how to download a project from the Scratch web site. In Chapter 6, we transformed a Scratch project to meet our own needs. In Chapter 9, we will give back to the Scratch community by making our own project available on the web site for others to enjoy and adapt.

In the process, we'll review the many ways in which we can promote our project to gain fans. For advanced users, we'll incorporate our Scratch projects on our own web server.

Real-world stimuli

We'll add our own personal touch to Scratch in Chapter 10 by connecting a webcam and a PicoBoard to our computer. The PicoBoard is an add-on piece of hardware that connects to our computer and delivers real-world stimuli to Scratch.

If you don't have a PicoBoard, you can still review this chapter to see what kinds of things you can do. Then, you can decide whether or not you want to get one. For example, this chapter gives us an example of how to program gravity that may be useful in your game whether you use a PicoBoard or not.

To demonstrate the board's light, sound, button, slider, and electrical resistance sensors, we will modify existing projects.

Summary

Imagine. Create. Share. It's the Scratch way. And now that we know that Scratch is good for our brains, let's get started with the installation.

2
Installation

As Scratch programmers, we have the freedom to choose the environment in which we operate. In this chapter, I'll enumerate the installation choices you have.

I'll assume you know how to install and download software on your computer, so instead of offering a step-by-step installation guide, we'll focus on special installation options.

In this chapter, we will:

- ◆ *Install Scratch on Windows, OS X, and Linux*
- ◆ *Run Scratch from a USB flash drive on Windows and OS X*
- ◆ *Ensure our browsers are configured to view Java web applications*
- ◆ *Review the Scratch license and distribution rights*
- ◆ Customize Scratch to work in networked environments

Sit down in front of your favorite operating system, and get on with the installation.

Install Scratch

From time to time, the Scratch team will release updated versions of Scratch. To download the latest version of Scratch for Windows, Mac OS X, or Linux, go to `http://scratch.mit.edu/` and follow the download link. You will be prompted to register first. Fill in all of the form's requested information or none of it, depending on your desired level of privacy.

Click the **Continue to Scratch Download** button to display the Scratch Download page.

Here, you can download the installer for your operating system, as shown in the previous screenshot. Feel free to skip ahead to your system.

Windows

For a normal Windows installation, we can download the Scratch installer, which guides us through the installation steps. When you launch the installer, Windows may complain that the Scratch installer is unsigned. You'll need to accept the message by clicking on the **Run** button, which implies you trust that the Scratch installer will not do harmful things to your computer.

If you have a version of Scratch installed, the installer removes the old version prior to installing the new version, which will cause you to lose any customized projects you may have saved to the Projects folder.

As you click through the installer, the only decision you have to make is where you want to install the Scratch program files. The default location is **C:\Program Files\Scratch**, but you can change it as needed.

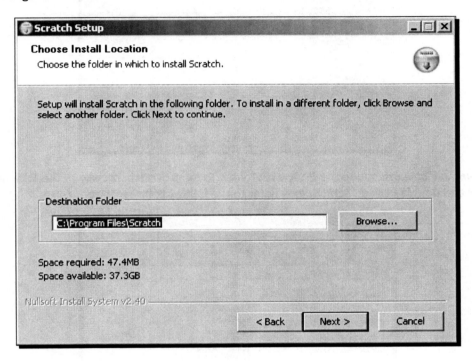

The installer will automatically launch Scratch after the installation finishes.

Run Scratch from flash drive

The Scratch team provides a ZIP file that contains all the program files we need to run Scratch, but it doesn't contain a point-and-click installer. The ZIP installation enables people who do not have administrator rights on their computers to install Scratch. We can also use the ZIP file to extract the Scratch program files to a USB flash drive for portable Scratch programming.

To get started, download the Windows ZIP file from the **Scratch Download** page. After the download completes, extract the files.

When prompted to choose a destination folder, enter the location of the flash drive. In my example, that's the **E:** drive.

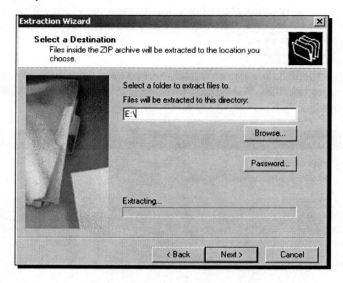

The files will be extracted to the **E:\Scratch** folder. To open Scratch, browse to the **E:\Scratch** folder and double-click on **Scratch.exe**. Refer to the following screenshot:

Integrate Scratch with the PortableApps.com suite

`PortableApps.com` provides a convenient way for users to run many popular open source applications, such as `OpenOffice.Org` and Firefox from a flash drive. The suite provides a menu of applications when you click on the **PortableApps.com** icon in the Windows system tray.

While the applications available directly from `http://www.PortableApps.com` have their own installers, adding Scratch to the menu is as simple as moving the Scratch program files to the `PortableApps` folder on the flash drive.

To make Scratch appear on the menu, extract the Scratch program files to the `PortableApps` folder. In my example, I have installed Scratch to **E:\PortableApps\Scratch**.

To make the PortableApps menu display the Scratch icon, open the **PortableApps** menu, and then select **Options | Refresh App Icons**.

Installation on Macintosh

The Mac OS X install follows the standard Macintosh installation procedures. Download the Mac OS dmg image from the Scratch Download page. Open the Scratch installer by double-clicking on the file you have downloaded. To install, drag the `Scratch` folder onto the `Applications` folder.

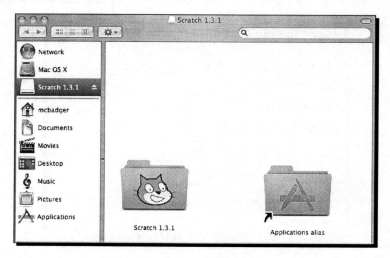

The installer creates a **Scratch** folder within the **Applications** folder. To launch Scratch, navigate to the **Applications | Scratch** folder and double-click on **Scratch.app**.

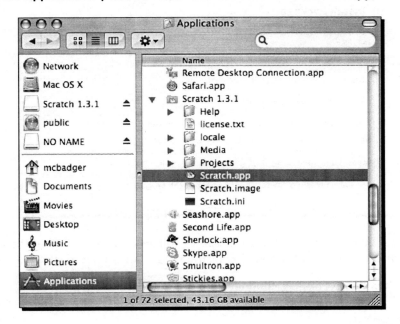

Run Scratch on USB flash drive

Like the Windows version, the OS X version of Scratch can be installed on a flash drive. Instead of dragging the Scratch installer to the Applications folder, drag it to the flash drive instead. This creates a Scratch folder on the flash drive.

Installation on Linux

At the time of this writing, the Scratch team provided a source install and a binary installer for Debian systems, such as Ubuntu. These versions are considered experimental. Linux users can also run Scratch using the Windows application loader Wine (www.winehq.org). Let's take a look at an Ubuntu 8.10 installation and then a Wine installation.

Download the Ubuntu installer from the **Scratch Download** page. After the download completes, double-click on the file you have downloaded to open the **Package Installer**, and then click on **Install Package**.

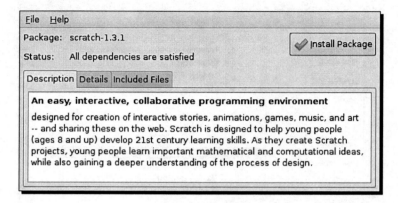

Enter your password when prompted, and Scratch will begin the installation. The installer puts a Scratch icon in the **Applications | Education** menu. Click on it to launch Scratch.

If the application doesn't display, continue with the troubleshooting problem.

Troubleshooting

When we launch the application from the menu icon, Ubuntu suppresses the error messages; therefore, we need to open a terminal window to get a handle on the problem. Try to launch the application by typing the command `scratch`.

Chances are you're encountering an error that says the **aoss package can't be found**.

To install the `aoss` package, open the **Synaptic Package Manager** from the **System | Administration** menu. When you do a search for "aoss" you'll find the package `alsa-oss`, which is an **Advanced Linux Sound Architecture (ALSA)** wrapper for **Open Source Software (OSS)** applications. You can read the package description if you'd like, but basically this package helps Scratch play sound.

Mark the package for installation. Then apply the changes to install alsa-oss. Now, Scratch will open when you launch it from the **Applications | Education** menu.

Or, you can just type `sudo apt-get install alsa-oss` at the command prompt, providing your password as needed.

Limitations

As you might expect with an experimental package, we can anticipate some problems. The biggest problem at the time of this writing was with the sound components of Scratch. You can check the current status at `http://info.scratch.mit.edu/Linux_installer`.

If you don't want to deal with experimental versions of Scratch, try Wine.

Wine and Scratch

If you need a more stable version, the Windows version of Scratch runs fine on Linux using the Windows application loader, Wine. Follow these steps:

1. Install the Wine package via Synaptic.
2. Download the Windows installer from the Scratch Download page.
3. Open a terminal window and run the command:
    `wine Desktop/ScratchInstaller*`
    -   This command assumes you're working from your home directory and you have downloaded the installer to your desktop.
4. From here, the Scratch installer looks just like it does on native Windows. Follow the default installation choices.

Double-click the Scratch icon on your Ubuntu desktop to open Scratch.

Confirm Java install

We don't need Java to develop Scratch programs, but we do need Java to view our projects on the Web. Most people's web browser will be configured to run Java already, so let's quickly test our browser setup.

Open your web browser and go to `http://javatester.org`. Click on the link at the top of the page that says, **Test the version of Java your browser is using**.

If Java is correctly installed, you will see your version of Java inside a pink rectangle, as shown in the following screenshot:

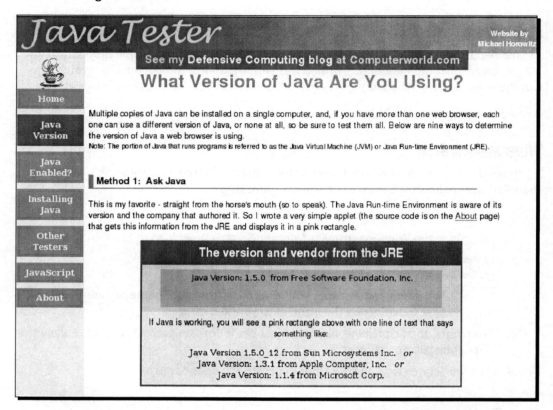

If the test indicates that Java is installed, you're done messing around. If you don't have Java installed, then you need to install it. Windows and Mac users can visit http://www.java.com to download and install the version for your operating system.

Ubuntu users can use Synaptic to install Java from the Ubuntu software repositories. Alternatively, the command `sudo apt-get install sun-java6-jre` will install Java support.

Customize your Scratch installation

Scratch 1.4 includes several options to help you customize Scratch for networked environments found in many schools, community centers, and other learning environments. In order to set these custom options, you must edit the Scratch.ini configuration file, which can be found in the root of the Scratch installation.

On a default installation, you will find the Scratch.ini file at
`C:\Program Files\Scratch\Scratch.ini`.

The following table includes a list of several customizations that you could deploy in your Scratch installations.

Customization	Example Scratch.ini options	Description
Disable the share button	Share=0	By default, users have the ability to share projects to the Scratch web site. This option disables sharing.
Hide network and local drives	VisibleDrives=Y:,Z:	The VisibleDrives option restricts access to the drives specified. If the VisibleDrives option is not set, users can see all drives connected to the computer.
Set custom home folder	Home=Y:\students* Home=Y:\students	Change the user's home project directory to the location specified. If you want each student to have an individual folder, use an asterisk in the folder path. The asterisk will be changed to the individual's user name. If you want each user to share a projects folder, do not specify an asterisk in the folder path.
Connect to a proxy server	ProxyServer=192.168.1.125 ProxyPort=9100	Scratch can be configured to connect to a proxy server by specifying the server address of the proxy server and the port number. Contact your network administrator for these values.

To change the default Scratch options, add the configuration to the Scratch.ini. The following screen shot shows an example Scratch.ini.

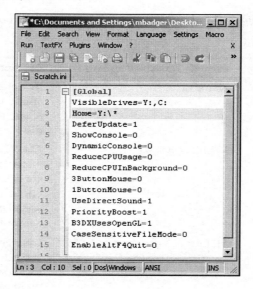

In the screen shot, the Scratch.ini limits access to the C: and Y: drives and sets a new home folder.

Redistribute Scratch freely

Put Scratch on a flash drive or burn it to a CD and give it away to your friends, students, and colleagues. Scratch encourages sharing as long as you abide by the license.

You can view the entire Scratch license online at `http://info.scratch.mit.edu/ Scratch_License`. In short, this license grants you the right to distribute Scratch and all its supporting materials, including media files and documentation.

If you do distribute Scratch, you must include the license file and this statement: "Scratch is developed by the Lifelong Kindergarten group at the MIT Media Lab. See `http://scratch.mit.edu`"

Source code license

Scratch is written in **Squeak**, an open source implementation of the Smalltalk-80 language. The Scratch source code is available under a second license that grants you the right to modify and distribute the source code as necessary, including derivative works. You can view the license information online at `http://info.scratch.mit.edu/Source_Code`. Here's a summary of the license:

- ◆ You cannot include the word "Scratch" in the name of the derivative work, except to say, "Based on Scratch from the MIT Media Laboratory."
- ◆ You must remove the official and trademarked Scratch logo and cat from derivative works.
- ◆ You cannot make the derivative work upload projects to the Scratch web site.

Share alike

All Scratch projects available on the Scratch web site and the sample projects included with the installation are available under the **Creative Commons Attribution-Share Alike** license. This license grants other Scratch users the right to copy and remix the Scratch projects.

Any derivative work you create from a Creative Commons licenses project will also be licensed under the Creative Commons Attribution-Share Alike license. Likewise, any project you make available on the Scratch web site will be licensed to share, including any image files.

As the license implies, you need to attribute your derivative work, as in "this project based on the Pong project by the Scratch sample projects team." That way, you give proper credit to the original author.

For more information on Creative Commons,
visit `http://creativecommons.org/licenses/by-sa/3.0/`.

Summary

With Scratch installed on your operating system of choice, let's scratch that programming itch. In Chapter 3, we'll take a high-speed, hands-on tour of Scratch and its capabilities.

3

Start Scratching

The anticipation of learning a new programming language can sometimes leave us frozen on the starting line, not knowing what to expect or where to start. In this chapter, we will:

- *Take a tour of the Scratch interface*
- *Create a couple of sample projects*
- *Learn some basic Scratch programming concepts*
- *Get our minds racing*

Our specific objectives include:

- *Learning how to work with Scratch*
- *Learning basic Scratch programming commands*
- *Finding inspiration to fuel our creativity*

Before we create any code, let's make sure we speak the same language.

The interface at a glance

When we encounter software that's unfamiliar to us, we often wonder, "Where do I begin?" Together, we'll answer that question and click through some important sections of the Scratch interface so that we can quickly start creating our own projects.

Now, open Scratch and let's begin.

Time for action – first step

When we open Scratch, we notice that the development environment roughly divides into three distinct sections, as seen in the following screenshot. Moving from left to right, we have the following sections in sequential order:

- Blocks palette
- Script editor
- Stage

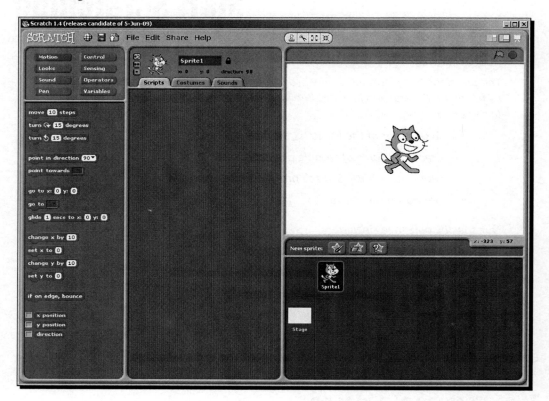

Let's see if we can get our cat moving:

1. In the blocks palette, click on the **Looks** button.
2. Drag the **switch to costume** block onto the scripts area.
3. Now, in the blocks palette, click on the **Control** button.
4. Drag the **when flag clicked** block to the scripts area and snap it on top of the **switch to costume** block, as illustrated in the following screenshot.

How to snap two blocks together?

As you drag a block onto another block, a white line displays to indicate that the block you are dragging can be added to the script. When you see the white line, release your mouse to snap the block in place.

5. In the scripts area, click on the **Costumes** tab to display the sprite's costumes.

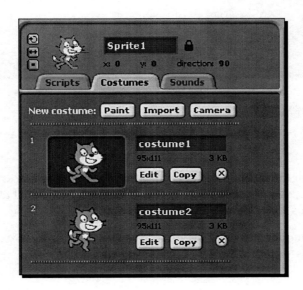

6. Click on **costume2** to change the sprite on the stage. Now, click back on **costume1** to change how the sprite displays on the stage.

7. Directly beneath the stage is a sprites list. The current list displays **Sprite1** and **Stage**.

8. Click on the sprite named **Stage** and notice that the scripts area changes. Click back on **Sprite1** in the sprites list and again note the change to the scripts area.

9. Click on the flag above the stage to set our first Scratch program in motion. Watch closely, or you might miss it.

What just happened?

Congratulations! You created your first Scratch project. Let's take a closer look at what we did just now.

As we clicked through the blocks palette, we saw that the available blocks changed depending on whether we chose **Motion**, **Looks**, or **Control**. Each set of blocks is color-coded to help us easily identify them in our scripts.

The first block we added to the script instructed the sprite to display **costume2**. The second block provided a way to control our script by clicking on the flag.

 Blocks with a smooth top are called **hats** in Scratch terminology because they can be placed only at the top of a stack of blocks.

Did you look closely at the blocks as you snapped the control block into the looks block? The bottom of the **when flag clicked** block had a protrusion like a puzzle piece that fits the indent on the top of the **switch to costume** block.

As children, most of us probably have played a game where we needed to put the round peg into the round hole. Building a Scratch program is just that simple. We see instantly how one block may or may not fit into another block.

 Stack blocks have indents on top and bumps on the bottom that allow blocks to lock together to form a sequence of actions that we call a **script**.

A block depicting its indent and bump can be seen in the following screenshot:

When we clicked on the **Costumes** tab, we learned that our cat had two costumes or appearances. Clicking on the costume caused the cat on the stage to change its appearance.

As we clicked around the sprites list, we discovered our project had two sprites: a cat and a stage. And the script we created for the cat didn't transfer to the stage.

We finished the exercise by clicking on the flag. The change was subtle, but our cat appeared to take its first step when it switched to costume2.

Basics of a Scratch project

Inside every Scratch project, we find the following ingredients: sprites, costumes, blocks, scripts, and a stage. It's how we mix the ingredients with our imagination that creates captivating stories, animations, and games.

Sprites bring our program to life, and every project has at least one. Throughout the book, we'll learn how to add and customize sprites.

A sprite wears a costume. Change the costume and you change the way the sprite looks. If the sprite happens to be the stage, the costume is known as a background.

Blocks are just categories of instructions that include **motion**, **looks**, **sound**, **pen**, **control**, **sensing**, **operators**, and **variables**.

Scripts define a set of blocks that tell a sprite exactly what to do. Each block represents an instruction or piece of information that affects the sprite in some way.

We're all actors on Scratch's stage

Think of each sprite in a Scratch program as an actor. Each actor walks onto the stage and recites a set of lines from the script. How each actor interacts with another actor depends on the words the director chooses. On Scratch's stage, every object, even the stone in the corner, is a sprite capable of contributing to the story.

As directors, we have full creative control.

Pop quiz

1. Which of the following items are in each Scratch project?

   ◆ Sprite

   ◆ Stage

   ◆ Script

   ◆ All of the above

2. The **switch to costume** block is a what kind of block?

   ◆ Motion

   ◆ Control

   ◆ Looks

   ◆ Sensing

Time for action – save your work

It's a good practice to get in the habit of saving your work. Save your work early, and save it often:

1. To save your new project, click the **disk** icon at the top of the Scratch window or click **File | Save As**.

2. A **Save Project** dialog box opens and asks you for a location and a **New Filename**.

3. Enter some descriptive information for your project by supplying the **Project author** and notes **About this project** in the fields provided.

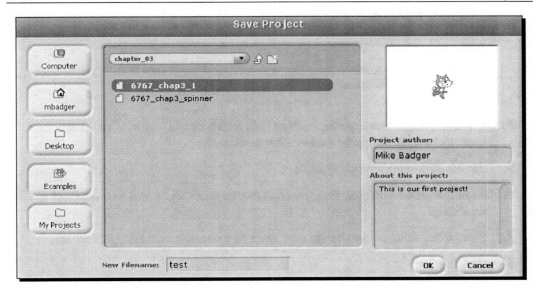

Set the cat in motion

Even though our script contains only two blocks, we have a problem. When we click on the flag, the sprite switches to a different costume and stops. If we try to click on the flag again, nothing appears to happen, and we can't get back to the first costume unless we go to the **Costumes** tab and select **costume1**. That's not fun.

In our next exercise, we're going to switch between both costumes and create a lively animation.

Time for action – a big step

We will continue working with our script from the previous example:

1. From the blocks palette, select **Motion**.

2. Drag the **change x by** block to the script area for **Sprite1** and snap it in place at the end of the script. See the following screenshot for reference:

3. Double-click on the script and watch your sprite move across the stage.

 Double-clicking on the script runs through each block of the script.

4. The **change x by** block has an number field with a default value of **10**. This number controls how far the sprite moves. Change **10** to **20**.

5. Double-click on the script again.

6. From the **motion** palette, drag the **change y by** block and add it to the end of your script.

7. Change the value in the **change y by** block to a negative number, such as **-30**.

8. Click the flag.

What just happened?

We added the **change x by** block to our script to make the cat move horizontally toward the right side of the stage. As we increased the value, our sprite moved further across the stage each time.

Next, we added the **change y by** block and gave it a negative value. When we clicked the flag, the sprite continued to move horizontally to the right, but it also moved down.

> The numeric x or y values found on several of the motion blocks measure pixels. The stage is 480 pixels wide and 360 pixels tall.

Coordinating a sprite's location

Scratch uses an **X** and **Y** axis to divide the screen into quadrants. Enter a positive number for X, and the sprite moves to the right. Similarly, enter a negative number for X, and the sprite moves to the left, or backward. A positive Y value makes the sprite climb, while a negative Y value makes the sprite fall.

The unit of measure on our coordinate system is pixels. Each sprite on the stage has an **X** and **Y** coordinate that allows you to locate it, but it also allows you to send a sprite to a specific coordinate.

As we'll discover later, even the mouse pointer has an X and Y coordinate that allows us to precisely locate the pointer.

Double-click control

So far we've seen two ways to control the sprite on the stage. We can build a script that uses a control block, such as the flag. Or we can double-click on a block or set of blocks to run a command on the sprite.

The ability to run an individual block against a sprite gives us a chance to observe the behavior of the block before we add the block to our script. It's a great way to test and learn.

Double-clicking on a block works if we have one, ten, or an infinite number of blocks stacked together.

Pop quiz

1. Double-clicking on a block or stack of blocks will run the script.

    ◆ True
    ◆ False

2. If you tell your sprite to **change x by -30** and **change y by 10**, which of the following statements best describes the motion of the sprite?

    ◆ 30 pixels right, 10 pixels up
    ◆ 30 pixels left, 10 pixels down
    ◆ 10 pixels left, 30 pixels up
    ◆ 30 pixels left, 10 pixels up

Time for action – in motion forever

So far the cat has moved incrementally across the screen by a set number of pixels and has stopped. Now, we're going to introduce the idea that the cat can stay in motion forever.

1. From the **Control** palette, drag the **forever** block onto the stack of blocks. Position it in such a way that it snaps in place between the **when flag clicked** and **switch to costume** blocks.

2. Double-click the stack of blocks and watch the cat disappear from the stage.

3. From the **Motion** palette, drag the **if on edge, bounce** block and snap it to the bottom of the **change y by** block. Now watch the cat reappear and bounce around the bottom-right corner of the stage.

4. Single-click on the script to stop the cat.

What just happened?

We wrapped our entire script in a forever block. In programming lingo, we put our script into a loop. However, that sent our sprite racing off the screen, so we had to tell our sprite to bounce when it hit the edge of the stage.

If you carried out the steps in the exercise as described, you noticed that as soon as you placed the **if on edge, bounce** block into your script, the sprite reappeared.

[You can add blocks to the loop and change the values as the script runs and the sprite automatically adjusts to the new values.]

Even though the sprite reappeared on the screen, it's trapped in the corner of the stage. It's stuck in a loop.

Loops play it again

Whenever we need to repeat an action or continually check for a condition within a program, we use a loop. The forever block represents an infinite loop. The blocks inside the loop will run as long as the Scratch program is running.

As we move through the book, we will encounter other types of loops. Examples include loops that run a set of blocks for a set number of times and loops that run only if a specified condition is met.

Time for action – get out of the corner

We need to get the cat out of the corner and moving across the stage in some kind of orderly fashion. We'll do that by replacing the **change x by** and **change y by** blocks:

1. Click on the scissors icon located on the toolbar above the stage to activate the scissors tool.

2. Move the scissors over the **change x by** block until it is outlined in a red square. Click your left mouse button to delete the block.

3. Similarly, delete the **change y by** block.

4. From the **Motion** palette, drag the **move 10 steps** block into your script and snap it in place before the **if on edge, bounce** block.

5. From the **Looks** palette, snap the **switch to costume** block into place after the **move 10 steps** block. Double-click the script to set it in motion. Select **costume1** from the list of costumes.

6. Add a second **switch to costume** block before the **move 10 steps** block. Select **costume2** from the list of costumes.

 The drop-down menu on the stack of blocks is sensitive. Click directly on the black triangle to display the available selections.

7. If the cat stopped moving, double-click the script again. It should be running upside down!

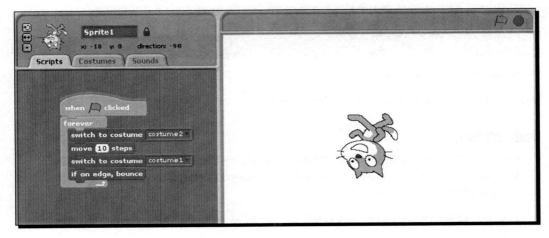

8. Let's change the rotation of the sprite. Informaton about the current sprite displays directly above the script area. To the left of the sprite are three directional buttons: **can rotate, only face left-right,** and **don't rotate.**

[Many buttons in Scratch will display a tool tip when you hover your mouse over the button. Try it with the rotation buttons.]

9. Click on the **only face left-right** rotation button, and now our sprite doesn't run upside down when it bounces off the side of the stage.

What just happened?

The **move 10 steps** block made the cat move in the direction it was facing, and when it bounced off the edge of the stage, the cat rotated so that it faced the other way. As the cat rotated, it turned upside down.

When we inserted the **switch to costume** block and set the value to **costume1**, the cat appeared to run. What really happened is that at every ten steps, our script displayed a different look as the cat moved across the screen. Our trick was subtle; as we changed the look of the cat, we created the appearance of running.

But we couldn't let the cat run upside down forever, so we adjusted the rotation so that when the cat hit the edge of the stage, it flipped 180 degrees and kept running.

Have a go hero

Make the cat run backward across the screen.

Hint: Set the rotation of the sprite to **don't rotate**.

Undo an action

If you deleted something you shouldn't have, there is an **Undo** button at the top of the Scratch window. Clicking **Undo** attaches the last block you deleted to your cursor, and you're able to snap it in place on the script.

You can only **Undo** the last action; Scratch doesn't have an unlimited undo capabilities.

Pop quiz

1. You need to stop your script before you can make changes to it.
    - ◆ True
    - ◆ False

2. Why do we use a forever block?
    - ◆ It adds a permanent block to the script
    - ◆ It means the script can't be changed
    - ◆ To execute a set of commands in a continual loop
    - ◆ To execute a set of commands while a certain condition exists

Add sprites to the stage

Earlier in the chapter, we learned that if we want something done in Scratch, we tell a sprite by using blocks in the scripts area. A single sprite can't be responsible for carrying out all our actions, which means we'll often need to add sprites to accomplish our goals.

We can add sprites to the stage in one of the following four ways: **paint new sprite, choose new sprite from file, get a surprise sprite**, or by **duplicating a sprite**. We'll duplicate a sprite in a future chapter. The buttons to insert a new sprite using the other three methods are directly above the sprites list.

Let's be surprised. Click on **get surprise sprite** (the button with the "?" on it.). If the second sprite covers up the first sprite, grab one of them with your mouse and drag it around the screen to reposition it.

If you don't like the sprite that popped up, delete it by selecting the scissors from the tool bar and clicking on the sprite. Then click on **get surprise sprite** again.

Each sprite has a name that displays beneath the icon. See the previous screenshot for an example. Right now, our sprites are cleverly named **Sprite1** and **Sprite2**.

Get new sprites

The **create new sprite** option allows you to draw a sprite using the Paint Editor when you need a sprite that you can't find anywhere else. You can also create sprites using third-party graphics programs, such as Adobe Photoshop, GIMP, and Tux Paint.

If you create a sprite in a different program, then you need to import the sprite using the **choose new sprite from file** option. Scratch also bundles many sprites with the installation, and the **choose new sprite** from **file** option will allow you to select one of the included files.

The bundled sprites are categorized into **Animals, Fantasy, Letters, People, Things**, and **Transportation**, as seen in the following screenshot:

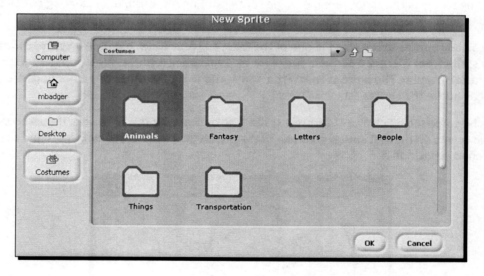

If you look at the screenshot carefully, you'll notice the folder path lists **Costumes**, not sprites. A costume is really a sprite.

If you want to be surprised, then use the **get surprise sprite** option to add a sprite to the project. This option picks a random entry from the gallery of bundled sprites.

We can also add a new sprite by duplicating a sprite that's already in the project by right-clicking on the sprite in the sprites list and choosing **duplicate** (command C on Mac). As the name implies, this creates a clone of the sprite.

The method we use to add a new sprite depends on what we are trying to do and what we need for our project. We'll use each of these methods as we move throughout the book.

Time for action – spin sprite spin

1. Let's get our sprites spinning.

2. To start, click on **Sprite1** from the sprites list. This will let us edit the script for **Sprite1**.

3. From the **Motion** palette, drag the **turn clockwise 15 degrees** block into the script for **Sprite1** and snap it in place after the **if on edge, bounce** block.

4. Change the value on the **turn** block to **5**.

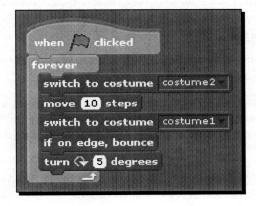

5. From the sprites list, click on **Sprite2**.

6. From the **Motion** palette, drag the **turn clockwise 15 degrees** block into the scripts area.

7. Find the **repeat 10** block from the **Control** palette and snap it around the **turn clockwise 15 degrees** block.

8. Wrap the script in the **forever** block.

9. Place the **when space key pressed** block on top of the entire stack of blocks.

10. From the **Looks** palette, snap the **say hello for 2 secs** block onto the bottom of the **repeat** block and above the **forever** block.

11. Change the value on the **repeat** block to **100**. Change the value on the **turn clockwise 15 degrees** block to **270**. Change the value on the **say** block to **I'm getting dizzy!**

12. Press the Space bar and watch the second sprite spin. Click the flag and set the second sprite on a trip around the stage.

What just happened?

We have two sprites on the screen acting independently of each other. It seems simple enough, but let's step through our script.

Our cat got bored bouncing in a straight line across the stage, so we introduced some rotation. Now as the cat walked, it turned five degrees each time the blocks in the forever loop ran. This caused the cat to walk in an arc. As the cat bounced off the stage, it got a new trajectory.

We told **Sprite2** to turn 270 degrees for 100 consecutive times. Then the sprite stopped for two seconds and displayed a message, **"I'm getting dizzy!"** Because the script was wrapped in a forever block, **Sprite2** started tumbling again.

We used the space bar as the control to set **Sprite2** in motion. However, you noticed that **Sprite1** did not start until we clicked the flag. That's because we programmed **Sprite1** to start when the flag was clicked.

Have a go hero

Make **Sprite2** less spastic. Instead of turning **270** degrees, try a smaller value, such as **5**.

Pop quiz

1. Which of the following is a way to add a new sprite to our project?
    - Paint a new sprite
    - Get a surprise sprite
    - Choose a new sprite from file
    - All of the above

Sometimes we need inspiration

So far, we've had a cursory introduction to Scratch, and we've created a few animations to illustrate some basic concepts. As we move through the book, we'll discover lots of other features as we create presentations, animations, and games. However, now is a good time to pause and talk about inspiration.

Sometimes we learn by examining the work of other people and adapting that work to create something new that leads to creative solutions.

When we want to see what other people are doing with Scratch, we have two places to turn. First, our Scratch installation contains dozens of sample projects. Second, the Scratch web site at `http://scratch.mit.edu/` maintains a thriving community of Scratchers.

Browse Scratch's projects

Scratch includes several categories of projects for **Animation**, **Games**, **Greetings**, **Interactive Art**, **Lists**, **Music and Dance**, **Names**, **Simulations**, **Speak up**, and **Stories**.

Time for action – spinner

Let's dive right in.

From the Scratch interface, click the **Open** button to display the **Open Project** dialog box, as seen in the following screenshot.

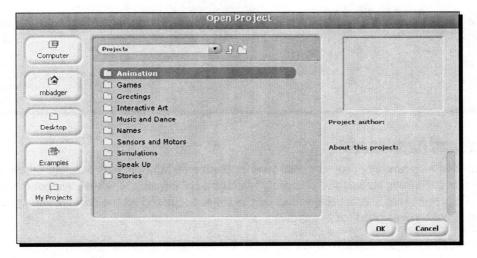

1. Click on the **Examples** button.
2. Select **Simulations** and click **OK**.

3. Select **Spinner** and click **OK** to load the Spinner project.

4. Follow the instructions on the screen and spin the arrow by clicking on the arrow.

5. We're going to edit the spinner wheel. From the sprites list, click on **Stage**. From the scripts area, click the **Backgrounds** tab. Click **Edit** on background number 1 to open the Paint Editor.

6. Select a unique color from the color palette, such as purple.

7. Click on the paint bucket from the toolbar, then click on one of the triangles in the circle to change its color. The paint bucket is highlighted in the following screenshot.

8. Click **OK** to return to our project.

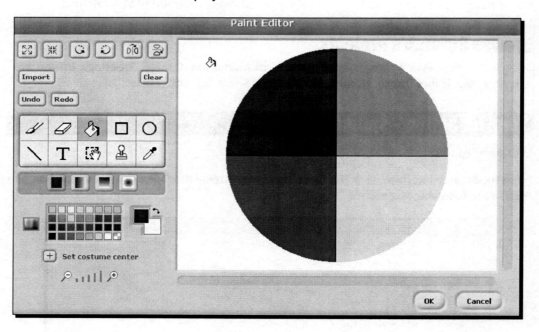

What just happened?

We opened a community project called Spinner that came bundled with Scratch. When we clicked on the arrow, it spun and randomly selected a color from the wheel. We got our first look at a project that uses a background for the stage and modified the background using Scratch's built-in image editor.

The Paint Editor in Scratch provides a basic but functional image editing environment. Using the Paint Editor, we can create a new sprite/background and modify a sprite/ background. This can be useful if we are working with a sprite or background that someone else has created.

Costume versus background

A costume defines the look of a sprite while a background defines the look of the stage. A sprite may have multiple costumes just as the stage can have multiple backgrounds.

When we want to work with the backgrounds on the stage, we use the **switch to background** and **next background** blocks. We use the **switch to costume** and **next costume** blocks when we want to manipulate a sprite's costume.

Actually, if you look closely at the available looks blocks when you're working with a sprite, you'll realize that you can't select the backgrounds. Likewise, if you're working with the stage, you can't select costumes.

Time for action – broadcast a message

We're going to continue spinning. Let's make the color wheel strobe as the arrow spins:

1. We need to duplicate the existing background. Select the **Stage** sprite and click on the **Backgrounds** tab in the script area. Click the **Copy** button to duplicate **background1**.

2. Now, let's flip the second background. For **background2**, click the **Edit** button to open the Paint Editor. Click the **Flip Horizontally** button that is located above the editor window and click **OK** to exit the Paint Editor.

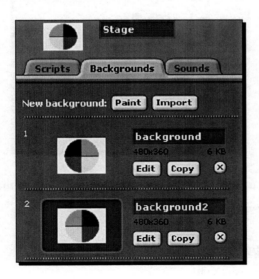

3. Select the **Spinner** sprite from the list of sprites.

4. We're going to program the sprite to send a message. From the **Control** palette, add the **broadcast** block to the script before the **turn 5 degrees** block. Click on the message drop-down list of the **broadcast** block and choose **New**.

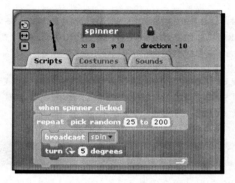

5. Type **spin** in the **message name** dialog box and click **OK**.

6. We're going to tell the stage to listen for the broadcast message. Select **Stage** from the list of sprites.

7. From the **Control** palette, add the **when I receive** block to the script area. Select **spin** from the message drop-down list.

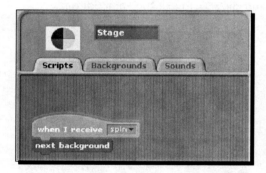

8. From the **Looks** palette, add the **next background** block to the script.

9. Click on the arrow.

What just happened?

Now we're programming in Scratch!

Our first step was to duplicate the existing background so we could flip it horizontally. We could have flipped the background vertically instead. Or, we could have flipped it both horizontally or vertically—it's a matter of whimsical choice.

We used a **broadcast** block on the **Spinner** sprite to let the stage know when we clicked the arrow. The arrow sent the message **spin**, which told the stage to switch to the next background, and this produced a strobe effect.

The stage knew how many times to switch backgrounds because when we clicked on the arrow, the script selected a random number between 25 and 200. In the original project, the random number controlled how many times the arrow spun around the circle.

In our new project, if the script selected a random number of 30, the following set of commands repeated 30 times in sequence: broadcast the message **spin** and turn to the right 5 degrees. For each spin, the background switched.

Broadcast messages coordinate sprites

When a sprite broadcasts a message, it's a clue to the other sprites that something should happen. In order for another sprite to react to the message, it needs to be told to listen for the broadcast message by using a **when I receive** block. Multiple sprites can be controlled with a single broadcast. If a sprite is not instructed to listen for a broadcast message, then it ignores the message.

You can think of broadcasts as a conversation starter. Conversations require two or more participants to engage. If I pass you on the street, I might say, "Hi, reader." Depending on the circumstances you might respond in one of three ways. First, you might say, "Hi, Mike." Second, you might wave. Third, you might ignore my message and continue on your path.

Pop quiz

1. When using the **pick a random number** block, how can we control what random number gets selected?

    ◆ Change the beginning number range
    ◆ Change the end range
    ◆ All of the above
    ◆ We can't control which random number gets selected

2. The **switch to costume** block and the **next costume** block always achieve the same result.

    ◆ True
    ◆ False

3. We use the **broadcast** block to do what?

- To enable one sprite to issue commands to another sprite
- To say a message on the screen
- To send a message to the other sprites
- To initiate a loop

Browse the Scratch community

Learning by doing is a great way to figure things out, but interacting with the code of other Scratch programmers provides an insight and an inspiration that you might not find on your own. If you visit the Scratch web site at `http://scratch.mit.edu/`, you can browse community projects by **Newest Projects**, **Featured Projects**, **Top Remixed Lately**, **Surprise Projects**, **Top Loved Lately**, **Top Downloaded Lately**, and **Top Viewed Lately**.

 To view the Scratch projects on a web page, you need a Java Runtime environment installed. Refer to Chapter 2 for some help installing Java.

Take some time and click through several projects so you get a broad sampling. As you view the work of others, stop thinking like a user and start thinking like a designer and a programmer. When you find something you like, ask yourself, "How does that work?" Then try to visualize how you might build the same thing. This exercise gets easier as you gain more experience.

Time for action – create an account

In order to download projects to our local computer, we need to create an account.

1. From the Scratch home page, click the **Signup** link to create an account or go to `http://scratch.mit.edu/signup`.

2. Enter all required information in the **Create an account** form.

3. Click the **sign up** button to create the account.

4. Read the terms of use at `http://scratch.wik.is/Terms_of_use`. It's a link in the page footer.

5. Welcome to the Scratch community.

What just happened?

We created an account at the Scratch web site. We'll learn how to share our projects in Chapter 9, but for now, we need an account so that we can download a project.

Abide by the terms of use

It's important that we take a few moments to read the terms of use policy so that we know what the community expects from us. Directly from Scratch's terms of use, the major points are:

◆ Be respectful
◆ Offer constructive comments
◆ Give credit
◆ Help keep the site friendly

Time for action – download a project

Without further hesitation, find a project you like and download it:

1. Click the link to download the project.

2. When prompted by your web browser, save the project to your computer.

3. Next, open the project in Scratch. From the Scratch interface, click on the **Open** button.

4. In the **Open Project** dialog box, navigate your filesystem and open the project you just downloaded.

What just happened?

We found a project we liked, we downloaded it, and then we opened it. As you review the project code in the Scratch interface, you can begin to answer the question, "How does it work?" You did remember to think like a designer and not a user, right?

Now that you saw the code, are you surprised by what you saw? Don't worry about whether or not you understand what it all means. You will.

Our mothers taught us to share, which brings us to the other implicit concept in this exercise. The Scratch community also encourages us to share, and each project on the Scratch web site is available under a **Creative Commons Attribution-Share Alike License**.

Creative Commons

The Attribution-Share Alike license is simple in concept and practice. When you find an interesting project, feel free to download it and remix it to create something new. Then credit the original author. The project notes make a great place to credit the work of others. By the time we finish this book, we will have several projects to share with the Scratch community, and we hope that our work inspires someone else to create something new and unexpected.

For more information about Creative Commons licensing, visit `www.creativecommons.org`.

Have a go hero

Modify the project you just created in some way. If you're not sure where to begin, try inputting different values into the blocks to see what happens.

There is no right way, just exploration.

Summary

Feel warmed up? This chapter helped us feel comfortable working with Scratch by covering some basic concepts. Each Scratch project contains sprites with costumes, scripts, blocks, and a stage with backgrounds.

In this chapter, we built a couple of sample scripts to demonstrate how we can control the sprites in a project. For example, we used motion to move the sprites, forever loops to keep the sprite moving, and broadcast messages to coordinate the actions of multiple sprites.

We finished up the chapter by sampling and remixing projects from Scratch's sample projects and from the Scratch web site. We also discovered that Scratch promotes sharing as a way to learn and encourage ideas.

Let's continue building our Scratch skills in the next chapter by working with graphics and slideshows to create a greeting card and a photo album.

4
Graphics and Slideshows

Now that we've taken a tour of Scratch and created some sample snippets of code, let's create our first project. We both have friends and family who have birthdays, even if they deny them. So in our first project, we will build an animated birthday card that we can send to mom, dad, a sibling, or a friend. In our second chapter project, we'll quickly put together a picture slideshow.

As we have fun creating our projects, we'll learn how to:

- ◆ *Create sprites using the Paint Editor*
- ◆ *Add images to our project*
- ◆ *Control the timing of our scripts*
- ◆ *Change the graphic effects of the images*

We start with a happy birthday wish.

Happy birthday wishes

Traditional birthday cards that you buy five minutes before a party seem like an impersonal way to show someone you care. So when you care enough to send a card, make it a homemade card that you designed. Instead of cutting, gluing, and stenciling paper, we're going to make a homemade animation in Scratch.

Can't think of anyone to send a card to? Send it to yourself—I won't tell.

Time for action – paint a happy birthday sprite

When we create a new project, our first task is to add our cast of characters and props. Otherwise, we won't have any sprites to animate. Let's start by adding the most obvious part of a birthday card: "Happy Birthday."

1. Open Scratch and click the **New** button to create a new Scratch project.

2. Delete the **cat** sprite. In the sprites list, right-click on the **cat** and choose **delete**.

3. Click on the **paint new sprite** button to display the Paint Editor.

4. In the **Paint Editor**, choose the **Text tool**.

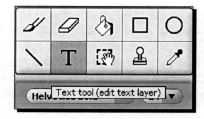

5. A vertical blue bar displays in the editor to indicate we are able to type. Type **Happy Birthday.**

6. If the text scrolls off the screen, use the horizontal and vertical scroll bars on the editor window to position the text in the editor window.

7. Let's change the font and size. Highlight the text, and choose a font from the font drop-down list.

8. Next select a font size. My example uses the font Ani, and I set the size to 36.

 The font drop-down list displays all the fonts that are installed on your system, so font selections will vary by user.

9. Now, change the text color. Select a color from the color palette. Happy Birthday now displays in the color you selected. Refer to the following screenshot:

10. Click on **OK** to close the Paint Editor and return to the stage.

The sprites list contains a new item labeled **Sprite1**.

What just happened?

We used the Paint Editor to create a simple, custom **Happy Birthday** sprite in the font, size, and color of our choosing.

Did you notice that as soon as you selected a new color, font, or size, the text immediately reflected your selection? The Paint Editor gave us a real-time preview of our work. When we clicked **OK** in the Paint Editor to save our sprite, the sprite on stage looked exactly as it did in the Paint Editor.

Interface design

As we build our projects, thinking about how we program our games and stories is only part of the creative process. We need to design our user interface. In every project we create, we will make design choices about how our users view and use our projects.

When we choose colors, fonts, and size, we make decisions about typography, which affects our project design. Where we place a sprite on the stage, how we take our user through our project, and how we control our sprites are all design decisions.

For a real-world example of design, take a close look at the pages of this book. The use of headings to navigate chapters and how each heading displays including font, size, and color is a design. The margins on the page and the use of white space affect how the page is laid out, which in turn affects how easily you can read the material. Numbered and bulleted lists are a design choice.

Feel free to experiment with the design of your projects until you find something that looks good to you. You can always refine it later.

Set the stage

A white background seems boring and we're not going to tolerate boring, are we? Let's see how easy it is to design our stage.

Time for action – paint the stage

Let's decorate our stage with a fresh coat of paint:

1. Select **Stage** in the sprites list.

2. Select the **Backgrounds** tab in the scripts area to show a list of backgrounds. Our project is new, so we see the default white background.

3. Open the stage in the Paint Editor by clicking on the **Edit** button.

4. Apply a fresh coat of paint by selecting the fill tool and then choosing a color. Click on the stage to fill it with the selected color.

5. Now, remove the color from the stage by pressing the **Clear** button located above the stage in the top-right corner.

6. Paint the stage with a gradient. With the fill tool and a color selected, choose a fill option from the options area.

7. The options area is located beneath the toolbar. As seen in the following screenshot, we have four fill options: 1) Fill the entire space 2) horizontal gradient 3) vertical gradient and 4) circle gradient.

 Use the flip horizontally and flip vertically buttons to change the orientation of the horizontal and vertical gradients.

8. On second thought, let's go back to a solid color on the stage. Clear the stage and use the fill tool with the solid color box selected in the options area. I'm going to use yellow.

9. Let's frame the stage in a second color. Click the **Shrink** button to make the current block of color smaller. An area of white space displays on the edge of the stage.

10. Paint the stage trim by selecting a new color from the color palette. With the fill tool selected, click anywhere in the trim area to fill it with the second color.

11. Click **OK** to save the background. Your stage should resemble the following screenshot:

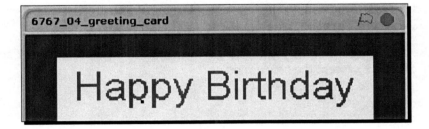

Don't like the current paint job? Feel free to redecorate. It is, after all, your card.

What just happened?

It took us a few tries to get the paint job and effect we wanted, but using the Clear tool made starting over a snap. We were able to try several fill colors including gradients with relative ease until we got the correct effect.

When we shrank the solid color of the stage, we created a white space that we filled with a second color. When we applied the second color, it filled only the white space because the original color formed a boundary that the fill wouldn't cross.

Were you thinking about design as you painted? If not, you may have been surprised by the result when you clicked **OK** to save the stage background. As we add sprites and designs to our projects, making sure everything integrates well will be one of our challenges.

You may need to change the color of the **Happy Birthday** sprite, which can be done by editing the sprite's costume, which can be found by clicking the **Costumes** tab.

Adding gradients

When we add a gradient with the Paint Editor, we create a gradual progression from a dark color to a light color. In Scratch, the horizontal gradient starts with the darkest shade at the left and progresses to the lightest shade at the right. With a vertical gradient, the darkest shade is on the right side. You can flip the gradients using the flip tool.

When you place a circle gradient, the center of the circle is where you clicked the mouse. The center is also the darkest shade in the gradient.

When working with gradients, the gradient will fill to a boundary. If the stage is empty, then the gradient will fill the entire space. If you draw a square in the middle of the stage and fill the square with a gradient, the gradient confines itself to the boundary of the square.

Have a go hero

Edit the stage background of your birthday card and apply a gradient to the center of the framed background. If you remove the framed background we created, use the **Rectangle tool** to draw a square. Then fill it with a gradient.

After you're done experimenting, you can cancel the Paint Editor to return to your previous design. Or, click **OK** to accept the new design.

Pop quiz

1. If you want to create a text sprite with the Paint Editor, what tool do you use?

    ◆ Fill tool

    ◆ Text tool

    ◆ Gradient tool

2. The gradient tool produces what kind of graphical effect?

    ◆ A block of color fades from light to dark shades

    ◆ A block of color alternates from light to dark shades like zebra stripes

    ◆ It draws a solid block of color with a dark center

Sprite costumes

So far, our project contains exactly one sprite that we created, but we do not want to create all of our sprites in the Paint Editor. Thankfully, Scratch bundles many sprites with the default installation that we can find in the Costumes folder.

 On a typical Windows installation, you can find the sprites at C:\Program Files\Scratch\Media\Costumes.

A costume gives the sprite its initial look. The default Costumes folder includes **Animals**, **Fantasy**, **Letters**, **People**, **Things**, and **Transportation**. In our next exercise, we use individual letters to display a message on the screen. This gives us more control over how we can display and animate the text.

Time for action – address the card

We have not placed one block of code in our birthday card. That will change soon enough, but we have one more graphic element to add. I'm sending my card to my mom, so I'm going to spell "Mom." You may choose anyone you want, but I'd recommend you to keep the name short for this exercise.

1. From the sprites list, click on **choose new sprite from file** to display the **New Sprite** dialog box.

2. We're going to spell out the word "Mom" using letters we find in the Costumes | Letters folder. Click on **Costumes**.

3. Double-click on the **Letters** folder to display a folder of letter types. Let's open the **funky** folder by double-clicking on it.

4. Scroll down the list of letters, select **M** and click **OK**. The letter **M** appears on the stage.

5. It's a good thing we didn't decide to spell "Happy Birthday" this way. Finish spelling "Mom" with letters from the funky letters folder.

6. Our letters are stacked on top of each other on the stage, so we need to move them around in order to read the word "Mom." Click on each letter and drag it to the preferred point on the stage.

What just happened?

"Happy Birthday, Mom." Now it's starting to look like a card. For the grammarians among us, feel free to insert a comma after birthday.

One letter at a time, we brought Mom to the stage. I don't know about you, but this exercise made me want to cheer. "Give me an 'M.' Give me an 'O'. Give me an 'M'."

Did you make an observation as you dragged each letter around the stage to correctly spell Mom? You dragged the "M," the "O," and the "M" independently of one another. We can't drag each letter in the **Happy Birthday** sprite around the stage. Go ahead, give it a try. You can move the entire phrase, but you can't separate Happy from Birthday.

Working with sprites

Take a look at your sprites list. It contains four sprites plus a stage.

The difference in our sprites comes from the way they were added to the project. We created the **Happy Birthday** sprite using the Paint Editor's Text tool. We set the display characteristics by choosing the font, color, and size. We can't edit Happy Birthday from the stage, but we can edit the text again later via the text editor.

When we added the funky font letters to spell "Mom", we really chose images from Scratch's library that represented a letter in the font. Think of it this way: We have one image on the stage that says "Happy Birthday", and every time we see that image, it will say "Happy Birthday."

On the other hand, we can position the O between the two M'S to spell mom, but we could just as easily arrange the images of the letters as MMO. But that would be nonsense.

This is just like the magnetic poetry kits that you can stick on the refrigerator. Sometimes the kit includes whole words or phrases. Other times, the kit comes with individual letters you must arrange to form words and phrases.

If you want to be able to animate and control each letter, you need to add images one at a time to spell the word.

Animating the card

This is the 21st century, and we can do much better than a card with static pictures. We want animation.

Time for action – hide all sprites

Before we start the animation, we will start with a blank screen by clearing the sprites from the stage. Then, we'll introduce and animate each sprite in turn. Let's send all the sprites backstage to wait until their lines come up.

1. Select the **Happy Birthday** sprite to display its script area.

2. From the **Looks** palette, drag the **hide** block into the script area.

3. We need a way to control when the **hide** block gets executed. From the **Control** palette, snap the **when flag clicked** block to the top of the **hide** block.

4. Hide each of the letters that spell Mom using the same script. Try the following short cut:

   ◆ Right-click on the **Happy Birthday** script and select **duplicate**. The script attaches to your mouse cursor.

   ◆ Drag the script to one of the other sprites in the sprites lists and click. The script copies to the sprite.

◆ Duplicate the script for the remaining sprites, with the exception of the stage.

5. Check your work. Click on each sprite and confirm it has the script that hides the sprite when the flag is clicked.

6. Click on the flag and watch our greeting, "Happy Birthday, Mom" disappear from the screen.

7. In the current state, you can make the sprites reappear by right-clicking on each sprite in the sprites list and choosing **show**.

What just happened?

As creative directors, we want control over when and how our sprites enter the stage. For this project, we don't want "Happy Birthday, Mom" passively sitting there, so we send them backstage.

The **when flag clicked** block we added to the script area for each sprite tells each sprite to do something when the flag is clicked. In our example, we tell them to hide, which clears each sprite from the stage.

In Chapter 3, we learned that we could duplicate backgrounds in the Spinner project. This time we used the duplicate tool to copy and paste blocks of code to the other sprites, which was quicker than building the same script one block at a time for each sprite.

Time for action – display happy birthday

Can you imagine mom's confusion? She clicks on the flag, and the screen goes blank. That's like going to a play where all the actors are sitting on the stage, in front of the curtain, until showtime. Then, when the curtain goes up, all the actors disappear. But we don't go to the theater to watch an empty stage. We want actors. Without further fuss, let's introduce our sprites:

1. Let's bring out the **Happy Birthday** sprite first. Select the **Happy Birthday** sprite from the sprites list.

2. From the **Control** palette, add the **wait 1 secs** block to the script.

3. Show the sprite by adding the **show** block from the **Looks** palette.

4. Run the script by clicking on the flag. Happy Birthday disappears and reappears one second later.

5. From the **Control** palette, snap the **forever** block in place below the **show** block.

6. From the **Looks** palette, drag the **change size by 10** block into the **forever** block.

7. Change the value on the **change size** block to **-20**.

8. Add a second **change by 10** block to the forever loop.

9. Change the value on the **change size** block to **20**.

10. From the **Looks** palette, add the **wait .5 secs** block between the two **change size** blocks.

11. From the **Control** palette, add a **broadcast** block between the **show** and **forever** blocks.

12. On the **broadcast** block, add a new message: **hi mom**.

13. Click the flag to make Happy Birthday pulsate on the screen.

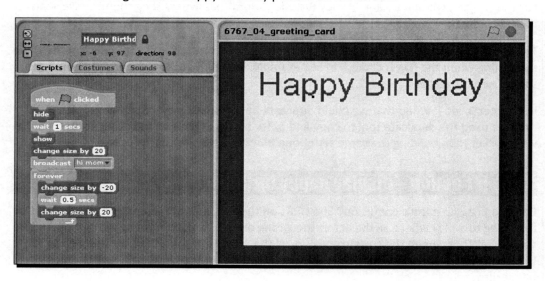

If you haven't already done so, you can stop your pulsating sprite by clicking on the **Stop** button.

What just happened?

Like a beating heart, Happy Birthday contracts and expands on the stage for as long as the script runs. We get the pulsating effect from the blocks of code in the forever loop. We increase the size by 20 pixels, and then half a second later we decrease the size by 20 pixels.

We can stop and start the script as many times as we want and Happy Birthday will not change size. But if we remove the first **change size by 20** block after the **show** block, our Happy Birthday message would get smaller each time we stop and start the script.

Before our sprite enters into its infinite loop, it broadcasts the message, **hi mom**. Nothing happened in our script as a result of the broadcast because nothing is set to receive the message.

Sprite names

Imagine if all the characters in Arthur Miller's *Death of a Salesman* were named Actor1, Actor2, Actor3, and so on. We'd lose track of the characters quickly. If we look closely at our list of sprites, we see the following names: Sprite1, Sprite2, Sprite3, and Sprite4. Let's give our sprites names, so they're as memorable as Willy Loman.

Time for action – roll call

Let's rename our sprites:

1. Select **Sprite1** from the sprites list.

2. Look at the Sprite Info section in the middle third of the screen. Next to the rotation buttons, the text **Sprite1** displays in an entry field.

3. Delete the text **Sprite1**.

4. Enter **Happy Birthday**.

5. Rename the remaining sprites with a memorable name, such as **First M**, **Second M**, and **O**.

Each sprite in the sprites list can now be identified by a unique name.

Choose appropriate names

To the computer, Sprite3 is just as good as First M, but humans benefit from associating sprites, costumes, backgrounds, lists, variables, and messages to descriptive names. In our example project, we spell Mom from individual sprites. How do we know if Sprite2 is the First M or the Last M? But if we rename Sprite2 to First M, we have no doubt.

In addition to providing context, names provide a way for us to easily identify our objects later. For example, if we broadcast one message as "message 1" and another as "message 2", we may not know which message does what when the time comes to make a sprite perform an action based on a message. If the message becomes "hi mom," then we know that the message signals the beginning of the mom animation.

Because meaningful names give us a context and understanding about the object, it helps us and other programmers understand our code later. Meanings may be fresh while we create our project, but what happens in two weeks or two months when we need to figure out what "message 1" controls?

As we create our projects, don't rely on Scratch's default naming. Change it as necessary.

Graphical transformations

We can change the appearance of a sprite very easily, as we have seen with the Happy Birthday card, and Scratch includes several special effects that we can apply directly to the sprite.

The effects in the following table can be found in the **change color effect by 25** and **set color effect to 0** blocks in the **Looks** palette:

Effect	What it does
color	Changes the color of the sprite.
fisheye	Distorts the sprite with a rounded edge as if you're looking at it through a glass or peep hole.
whirl	Twists the sprite around a center point and produces an effect similar to throwing a pebble in the water.
pixelate	Increases the size of the pixels in the image so that you can see them. Creates a blurry image.
mosaic	Splits the sprite into a pattern of smaller images of itself.
brightness	Increases the luminance of the sprite to make it appear brighter.
ghost	Makes the sprite transparent so that you can see other sprites and backgrounds through the sprite.

To apply more effect, increase the numeric value. You can also apply a negative-value to each effect.

Let's experiment with some graphic effects.

Time for action – give me an "M"

In the next act, we introduce Mom. The letters M, O, and M are currently hidden, so let's bring them out:

1. We're going to start with **Second M**. Select **Second M** from the sprites list so that we see the scripts area.

2. We will control the **Second M** sprite with the **when I receive hi mom** control block. Drag that block into the scripts area.

3. To display the letter M, we need to add the **show** block.

4. Click the flag to see the script run so far. As Happy Birthday beats on the screen, the second letter M appears on the screen.

5. Click the **stop** button when you're ready to continue.

6. From the **Control** palette, snap the **repeat 10** block to the bottom of the **show** block.

7. We're going to make the M a mosaic. From the **Looks** palette, add the **change color effect by 25** block to the repeat loop. Change the graphical effect from **color** to **mosaic** by selecting **mosaic** from the drop-down list.

8. Click the flag and watch the effect of our action. Our M is a mosaic, but it's no longer readable.

9. Click **Stop** when you're ready to continue.

10. From the Looks palette, double-click on the **clear graphic effects** block to redisplay the letter M.

11. Snap another **repeat 10** block to the bottom of the first **repeat 10** block.

12. Insert a second **change mosaic effect by 25** block into the new **repeat 10** block. Change the effect from **25** to **-25**.

13. Now we need the script to announce when it's finished. Add a **broadcast** block and create a new message **next m**.

14. Let's see what we've done. Click the flag.

The following screenshot shows the letter M as we apply the mosaic effect by 25:

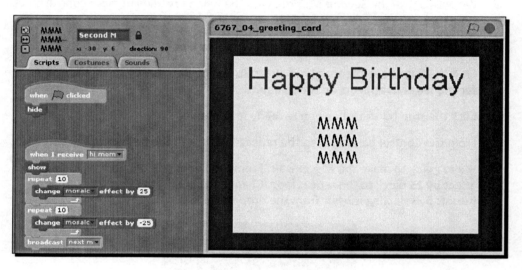

The following screenshot shows the finished product after we apply the **change mosaic effect by -25**:

What just happened?

Finally, we acknowledged the **Happy Birthday** sprite's "hi mom" broadcast message. "Hi mom" was the cue that told **Second M** to enter the stage with dramatic effect.

Once the letter M is displayed, it splits apart to form a pattern of little Ms before it reconstituted itself into a whole letter. The code that created our pattern was straight forward. First, we applied a mosaic pattern with an effect of -25 each time the **repeat** block ran. The effect repeated 10 times. The second **repeat** block also ran 10 times, but it changed the mosaic effect by -25 each time. The second **repeat** block undid the effects of the first **repeat** block.

Loop with repeat

Like the **forever** block, the **repeat** block creates a loop that runs the blocks inside the loop. The **repeat** block differs from the **forever** block in that we specify a number of times to run the loop.

In addition to entering a whole number in the **repeat** block, we can insert variables that represent numbers. We will review variables in Chapter 6.

Pop quiz

1. If you want to loop through a set of blocks for a specific number of times, which block do you use?

   ◆ Forever

   ◆ Repeat

   ◆ Broadcast

2. Which of the following graphical effects splits a sprite into a pattern of smaller images of itself?

   ◆ Whirl

   ◆ Pixelate

   ◆ Mosaic

3. How do you copy a script from one sprite to another?

   ◆ Right-click on the script, select **duplicate**, and drag the script to the second sprite

   ◆ Highlight the script, press Ctrl + C to copy it, and press Ctrl + V to paste it on the second sprite

   ◆ You can't copy scripts from one sprite to another

Incremental improvements

Programming in Scratch, like most creative endeavors, is an iterative process. That means we build our scripts one block at a time, and we can expect to make multiple versions until we get the results we want.

Our initial efforts may have a bug, which means our script doesn't perform as we expect it to. Bugs happen for any number of reasons and as we encounter a problem, we troubleshoot it. Throughout the book, we'll have many opportunities to troubleshoot our scripts, but let's focus mainly on efficiency.

Remember how, as we stepped through the exercise, we ran the **clear graphic effect** block to reset our sprite to its default state? In our code, we essentially cleared the graphic effect with the second repeat block because it did the opposite of what the first repeat block did.

If after we **change the mosaic effect by 25** for 10 consecutive times, we add the **clear graphic effect** block, we create a simpler script. We get the same results, and we have less points of failure to troubleshoot in the future.

The following screenshot shows the revised script for the **Second M** sprite:

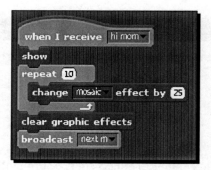

Time for action – give me another "M"

When we last left our script, the **Second M** in Mom displayed on the screen. Now let's display the First M in Mom.

The second letter M broadcast the message **next m**, so that is where we begin this exercise:

1. Add the **Control** block **when I receive next m** to the scripts area for the **First M** sprite.

2. Add the **show** block.

3. Let's rotate the M this time. From the **Motion** palette, add the **turn clockwise 15 degrees** block to the **show** block.

4. Click the flag to set the script in motion. Note that the first m is tilted 15 degrees. Click the **Stop** button when you've seen enough.

5. Wrap the **turn clockwise 15 degrees** block in a **repeat 10** block.

6. Change the input value on the **repeat** block to **25**.

7. Add a **broadcast** block and create a new message **gimme an O**. Click the flag to run the script and watch the M spin in place. Click **Stop** when you've seen enough.

Run the script multiple times. Note how the letter M has a different orientation each time the script runs.

What just happened?

Excited to get the call from the **Second M** sprite, **First M** tumbled onto the stage. The **repeat** block instructed the M to turn clockwise 15 degrees for a total of 25 times. Each time we click on the flag, the script starts from the M's position on the screen, which means the M will end at a different spot each time.

If we run our script enough times, our M inverts and looks like a W. That just won't do.

Time for action – set first M straight

To help ensure that the first M always displays in an upright position, we can undo the **turn clockwise 15** block with a **turn counterclockwise 15** block:

1. From the **Control** palette, add a **repeat 10** block.

2. Inside the **repeat 10** block, add a **turn counterclockwise 15** block.

3. Run the script several times.

What just happened?

We ensured that the first M always displays in the same position and therefore won't end up looking like a W. We used the technique earlier in the chapter, which is basically to create a duplicate block of code with a negative value to undo the first block of code.

This was certainly not the only way to solve the problem. For example, we could have added the **point in direction** block after the **show** block to accomplish a similar result.

Have a go hero – give me an "O"

We need only one more letter to spell the word Mom. The **First M** sprite is sending a broadcast "gimme an 'O'." Go ahead and display the letter O. If you need some help, look back at our previous exercise "Time for action–give me another 'M'."

Beware of gaudiness

Just because we can make our sprites rotate, pulse, and display in mosaic patterns doesn't mean we should apply all those effects at one time. In addition to animation, we also design through typography, color, and graphics. Animations are fun, but when every sprite moves in a seemingly random way, we may distract our user.

When you displayed the letter O in the hero exercise, did you animate O's entrance? If you animated the O with some type of look or motion, try removing it and use a **show** block with the **when I receive gimme an O** block. Evaluate the difference. The following screenshot shows how I display my letter O:

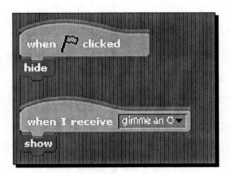

We make choices when we create our Scratch programs, and the choices we make benefit from some experimentation and inspection. Sometimes, we'll want the glitz while other times we'll prefer the simpler approach.

Time for action – give mom flowers

Let's put some finishing touches on our card for mom and add a vase of flowers:

1. Select the **choose new sprite from file** button in the sprites list.

2. Browse to **Costumes | Things**. Select the vase of flowers and click **OK** to add the flowers to the stage.

3. Scratch places the flowers in the middle of the stage, so we need to drag the vase to a place on the stage where it fits into the design.

4. We should add a personal note for mom on her birthday. Click the **Paint a new sprite** button to display the Paint Editor.

5. Type a personal note in any typeface and size you find appropriate. I like to joke with my mom, so for my message, I typed **So, I hear you're 29 again this year. I'm happy to say you don't look a day over 30.**

6. Click **OK** to add the new sprite to the stage. Again, you can position the sprite anywhere on the stage. You may even need to resize the sprite to make your message fit in a certain area.

7. To resize the sprite on the stage, select the shrink sprite tool from the toolbar. Click on the sprite you want to shrink. Repeat this step as needed.

8. Click the flag to display the card. Our animations continue to work, but the newly added sprites just stay on the stage. Click **Stop** when you've seen enough.

9. Let's try hiding the flowers and note for a couple seconds while our animation plays out. From the sprites list, select the **Flower** sprite.

10. Add the **when flag clicked** control box to the scripts area.

11. Instead of using the **hide** block, let's add the **change color effect by 25** block to the script.

12. Change color to ghost and change **25** to **100**.

13. From the **Control** palette, add the **wait 1 secs** block to the script, but change the value to **3**.

14. From the **Looks** palette, add the **clear graphic effects** block.

15. Click the flag to run the script. Now our flowers display three seconds after we click the flag and after the word Mom displays. Click the **Stop** button when you've seen enough.

What just happened?

We presented mom with a beautiful vase of flowers and she even laughed at the note. When we clicked the flag, we hid the flowers like we did with all the other sprites; however, we introduced the ghost effect with a value of 100. The net result is the same as the **hide** block.

The **wait 3 secs** block was a curious choice in that it departs from the broadcast messages we used to control sequence throughout the project. If the timing of the vase was important, having the O broadcast a message that the vase used as a signal to clear the graphic effects would be a better choice.

Ghosting an image

When we ghost a sprite we make it transparent so we can see whatever lies underneath. The higher the percentage we ghost the image by, the lighter it becomes. So, when we ghost an image by 100 percent, we make it invisible. In contrast, ghosting the image by a value of only 10 slightly fades the image.

Have a go hero

Change the graphical effects of the vase as it displays. Add the following blocks between the **wait 3 secs** block and the **clear graphic effects** block: **repeat 20, change ghost effects by -5,** and **wait 0.1 secs.**

After you have that working to your satisfaction, duplicate the code and copy it to the **Note** sprite.

Parallel execution

Each time we click the flag, we open a thread in Scratch. A thread is a programming concept that basically means when we launch two stacks of blocks at the same time, we perform concurrent tasks. For example, if we have four sprites, each using the **when flag clicked** block, we create four threads that run concurrently when the flag is clicked.

The obvious implication of this is that we can launch many activities from a single control. Even though we may need to open multiple threads at one time, we will likely have a sequence to enforce. To help coordinate how our sprites interact, we can use the **broadcast** and **when I receive** blocks.

Next steps

Sending mom a happy birthday card is nice, but don't forget about dad and the rest of the family. Actually, we could build cards for any occasion with Scratch: get well, thank you, happy anniversary, congratulations, and so on.

But why limit our imagination to greeting cards. We could turn this project into a party invitation.

In the next project, we will learn how easy it is to add our own photos.

Build a photo slideshow

It's easy to collect large amounts of digital pictures on our hard drives. For our next project, we're going to take a few photos and use Scratch to turn them into a slideshow to share with friends and family.

Before we begin, look through your photo library and identify a couple of photos for the show. If you don't have any photos, don't worry. Scratch includes some default backgrounds. I'll show you where they are in the first exercise.

Time for action – insert a title screen

Every presentation needs a title screen. Let's get started by creating a new Scratch project and deleting the cat:

1. From the sprites list, select the stage.

2. From the scripts area, click on the **Backgrounds** tab.

3. Import a new background by clicking on the **Import** button. The **Import Background** dialog box displays.

4. Browse the folders to select a background you like. I'm going to use the wooden-house from the Outdoors folder.

5. From the backgrounds list, delete the default background by clicking on the **X** next to the **Copy** button.

6. Open the background in the Paint Editor by clicking the **Edit** button.

7. Give the slideshow a name by using the Text tool to add text to the image. Look back to the Time for action–paint a happy birthday sprite exercise earlier in this chapter if you need help entering text. My slideshow is titled, **Buddy's Bottlecap Surgery**.

 When the Text tool is selected, you can position the text on the screen by grabbing the black square that appears in the top-left corner of the text area and dragging it around.

8. Click **OK** in the Paint Editor to save your work and return to Scratch.

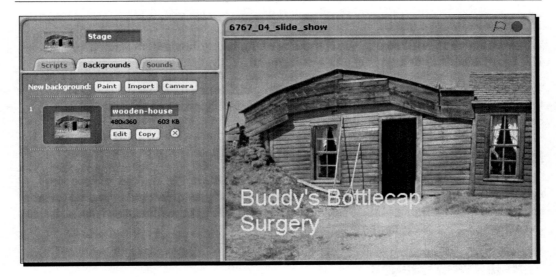

What just happened?

Every presentation needs a title screen, and we just created ours by importing a new background into our project. By now, it's clear that the Paint Editor is a central tool for us in Scratch, but did you notice a subtle difference in the way we added text?

Earlier in the chapter, we created a new sprite named Happy Birthday using the Text tool. This time, we added text to an existing image.

Time for action – import photos from disk

Let's import a batch of photos from our hard drives so that we have something to show:

1. From the **Backgrounds** tab of the stage, click **Import** to display the **Import Backgrounds** dialog box.

2. Browse your computer's folders until you find your photos. Add each photo to the project, one at a time.

Scratch uses the filename to identify the background in the list of backgrounds. You can rename your files with descriptive filenames (e.g., Fritz.jpg instead of img0004.jpg), so they're easily identified in your project.

3. To preview each image on the stage, click on it from the backgrounds list.

What just happened?

When we added the title screen, we chose one of the backgrounds from Scratch's library. This time we added our own image as a background.

Once we include the background image in our project, Scratch treats all the images the same. It doesn't matter if we use an included image, import an image, or paint our own background.

Image formats

Scratch imports the popular image formats such as PNG, BMP, JPG, and GIF. You can also import animated GIFs, but it will no longer be animated. If you import the animated GIF as a sprite, only the first frame of the animation is imported. To get the remaining frames, import the animated GIF as a costume for the sprite.

Working with images

Working with digital images is a topic worthy of its own book, but Scratch has some built-in image editing capabilities that we can use. Actually, we've been using Scratch's image editor in this entire chapter, and you may have observed that it has a limited feature set.

Basically, we can change colors, draw rectangles and circles, insert lines, type text, duplicate areas, resize, rotate, and flip. If we want more advanced editing capabilities, we need a more advanced editor, such as Photoshop, Fireworks, or GIMP.

Resize images

The stage in Scratch measures 480 pixels wide by 360 pixels high. In graphic design, we list the width first, so an 800 x 600 image is 800 pixels wide. If we were to look at an image under extreme magnification, we would eventually see individual dots. These dots are pixels, and they contain all the information the computer needs to display the image on the screen.

Counting pixels becomes important, so we can select images that will meet our needs. If we want an image to take up the entire background, we need an image that is at least 480 x 360 pixels to ensure that we have an acceptable image quality.

The problem with using an image that is less than 480 x 360 pixels is that we need to stretch or upsize the image in order for it to fill the screen. As we increase the size of an image, the pixels are made bigger, and we will begin to see the individual pixels. This effect creates a grainy and unclear image, which is often referred to as a **pixelated image**.

The good news is that if we start with an image that is larger than 480 x 360, then we don't need to resize the image at all. Scratch will resize the image to the correct dimensions automatically. We don't have to worry about image pixelation when we decrease the size of an image. Bottom line, always start with a larger image and downsize if needed.

How to measure images

In Scratch, we have two ways to determine if our image is big enough. On one hand, you can use the simple approach. If you display the background on the stage and any portion of the stage is still visible, then it means the image is too small. This method works, but it is not very precise.

Alternatively, the **Backgrounds** tab displays the size in pixels below the image name, as seen in the following screenshot:

If you look closely at the screenshot, you'll see my image is 480 x 320. It's 40 pixels too short! For now, it's not a big deal. I'll leave the white background display, but I could use the Paint Editor to fill that space with a solid color if I wanted to.

Time for action – flip through the photos

Now that we have our photos imported into Scratch, we will add a control to flip through them:

1. From the **Control** palette, drag the **when space key pressed** block to the scripts area of the stage.

2. Change the value from **space** to **right arrow**.

3. When we press the right arrow key, we want to advance the slideshow to the next photo. From the **Looks** palette, add the **next background** block to the **when right arrow key pressed** block.

4. Give it a try. Press the right arrow key until you've cycled through all the photos.

5. Let's add the ability to start over. Drag another **when space key pressed** block into the scripts area.

6. From the **Looks** palette, add the **switch to background** block to the **when space key pressed** block.

7. Change the background name on the **switch to background** block to be the title screen. My title screen is **wooden-house**.

8. Give it a try. Press the right arrow one or two times. Then press the Space bar to return to the title screen.

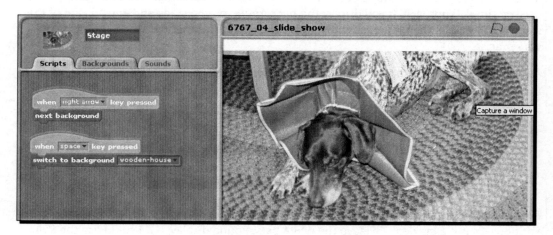

What just happened?

My dog Buddy had to have a bottle cap surgically removed from his stomach, and in exchange for his vet bill, I got to take pictures of his recovery. I like to share the photos and tell the story about how the only things visible on his X-ray were his ribs and a round bottle cap. It was like a cartoon.

When we got home, Buddy had to wear a cone around his neck to stop him from licking his incision. We made the little dog, Fritz, put the cone on, just for fun.

I can pause on each screen and reminisce for as long as I want to. When I'm ready to move on to the next photo, I press the right arrow key. The right arrow key always loads the next image, but if I want to start my story over, I press the space key.

We did not, however, build the script to view the previous image. That's because Scratch doesn't offer a previous background block. With some experimentation, we could probably come up with a way to go back through the slides, one photo at a time.

To change the order in which the photos appear, drag the photos up and down background list, which is similar to how we can arrange the costumes for a sprite.

Have a go hero

Give the photos in your slideshow a little style. Rotate one or more of the photos in your show on the stage.

Hint: Use the rotate clockwise and rotate counterclockwise tools in the Paint Editor.

Building audience participation

When it comes to controlling the action in our projects, there are multiple options. For example, the greeting card uses time and broadcast messages to direct the flow. Once the user starts the program, the user sits back and watches the animation from start to finish. It is completely automated.

It's comparable to sitting in the audience of a Broadway play. Once the curtain goes up, the actors enter the stage and the story unfolds with us as passive participants. This is a fine way to watch a play. But what if you could get out of your seat, go up to the stage, and inject yourself into the story? With Scratch, we can let the audience become active participants so that their input affects how the project plays out.

The slideshow uses keystrokes to control the action. If we want to view the next photo, we press the right arrow key. In other words, this is a completely manual approach. The slideshow doesn't advance without human interaction.

As we build our projects, we decide how much audience participation we want and we build our project that way. No wrong answer exists.

Time for action – present your show

Until now, we've been viewing our projects in the Scratch editor with the blocks palette and script areas visible. Let's check out Scratch's full screen mode:

1. Find the **Switch to presentation mode** button, located directly above the stop sign. It's the right-most button. See the following screenshot:

2. Click the **Switch to presentation mode** button to display your project in full screen.

3. Go through your slideshow with the right arrow key and the space bar.

4. When you're finished in presentation mode, press the **Esc** key on your keyboard to return to the Scratch interface. You can also click the **Exit presentation mode** button.

Pop quiz

1. How big is Scratch's stage?
    ◆ 360 x 480
    ◆ 480 x 360
    ◆ 420 x 320

2. Which of the following image formats does support?

 ◆ PNG

 ◆ GIF

 ◆ JPG

 ◆ All of the above

Next steps

I'm intentionally keeping the slideshow simple, but that doesn't mean you have to! A timed presentation with captions would make a nice upgrade to this script. Maybe add in some graphic effects each time the next background loads. A cartoon presenter who narrates each photo with a voice bubble could also be a fun variation.

As we worked through our slideshow, did you make the comparison to Microsoft PowerPoint or OpenOffice.org Presentation? Imagine how easily you could build an animated presentation to display last quarter's sales figures or present interactive poetry to your class.

Summary

Congratulations on creating your first two Scratch programs. If you're like me, you have more project ideas floating around your head than you can possibly process. That's part of what makes Scratch so fun. It's easy to turn ideas into projects, in part because everything we need is available within Scratch.

We introduced design as a central concept to our Scratch projects because so much of what we do is visual. As you create future projects, you should experiment with typography, graphic effects, motion, and design in order to get the most out of your project. Don't be afraid to answer the question, "What happens if I ... ?"

Of course, design only gets us so far. We needed to animate our sprites, so we worked with control blocks to start and stop the action and develop timing. Through our scripts, we manipulated the looks and motion, which further affected the design.

Now, you may be wondering how to share your projects. If you can't wait, jump to Chapter 9 and find out how. Then, come back to Chapter 5 to create a barnyard humor book that focuses on language and text.

5
Storytelling

Building on the design and graphic elements we learned in Chapter 4, we will animate a barnyard humor book. We'll use the animals to find our funny bone, and in the process, we'll get a great introduction to systematically creating a sequence of scenes that fit together.

In addition to practicing your storytelling skills, you'll learn how to:

- *Change the appearance of our sprites using costumes*
- *Convey speech*
- *Position our sprites using coordinates and motion*
- *Apply sound effects to our scripts*

We'll continue building upon the control techniques we learned in the previous chapters to organize the flow of the project with backgrounds, user clicks, and broadcast messages.

Are you ready to laugh and learn? Let's get started.

Barnyard humor

Let's spin some barnyard humor that's fit for users of all ages. Got a good joke or two? Feel free to substitute them for my example.

Table of contents

Our first step is to create a table of contents that users can use to navigate the jokes in our book.

Time for action – create TOC

To begin with, our book will have a chapter for a dog and a horse. We need to create clickable sprites to load into each chapter when we click on the entry in the table of contents.

1. Let's create a new sprite by clicking on the **paint new sprite** button in Scratch.

2. We need to add a button from Scratch's image library. From the Paint Editor, click the **Import** button to display the **Import Image** dialog box.

3. Navigate to **Costume | Things** and select **button**. Click **OK** to add it to the Paint Editor's canvas.

4. Use the Text tool to type **Dog** in any font you want.

5. Resize the text and position the word **Dog** so that it fits inside the button. Don't make the button bigger or else you will compromise its quality.

6. Click **OK** to save your work and add the new sprite to the project.

You can position the button anywhere on the screen, as shown in the previous screenshot.

What just happened?

We added the word **Dog** to a button to create our first table of contents entry. Using the Paint Editor, we imported a button sprite and then we layered text over it. When viewed on the stage, it displayed as a single button.

Have a go hero

Finish adding the following sprites to the table of contents page. Create a second button and label it "Horse." Then, create a heading that says "Table of Contents." Add a set of instructions that says, "Click an animal name to begin."

The Table of Contents heading and the instructions do not need to be placed on a button because we will try not to click on them during our project.

Feel free to experiment with your text or change it entirely. From this point onward, I'll assume you're working with a dog and a horse. However, if you want to work with a duck and a donkey, you won't hurt my feelings.

Add pages to our book

Now that we have a table of contents, let's add the corresponding pages.

Time for action – add new pages

Next, we are going to add two backgrounds to our project to represent pages in our book. This topic, from the picture slideshow project in Chapter 4, should be familiar to you. However, this time we will integrate a sprite with a background.

With the stage selected, let's get started:

1. We need a background for the horse. From the **Backgrounds** tab, click **import**.

2. Choose the **hay_field** image from the **Outdoors** folder.

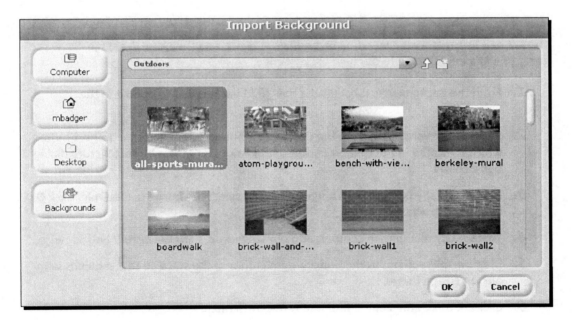

3. Our dog prefers a bed to hay. Import the **bedroom1** image from the **Indoors** folder.

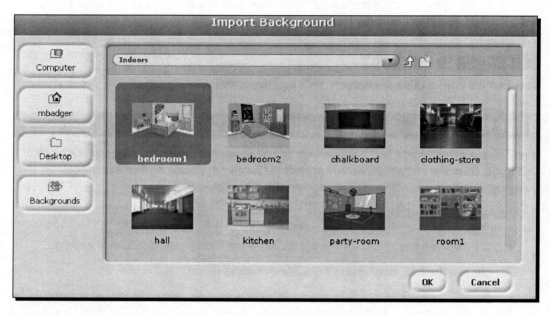

The animals in our story are stand-up comedians at heart, and they love the stage. So, we're going to add a microphone to our new backgrounds:

1. From the **Backgrounds** tab, edit the **hay_field** background to open it in the Paint Editor.

2. Import the microphone from the **Costumes | Things** folder. Click the **Import** button, which is located in the top-left corner of the Paint Editor. The **Import Picture** dialog box displays.

3. Navigate to the **Costumes | Things** folder and select the image named **mic.** Click **OK** to add the image.

4. That's a big microphone compared to our landscape. Click the **Shrink** button twice.

5. Drag the microphone to the bottom-right corner of the stage so that it blends with our landscape better.

6. Click **OK** to exit the Paint Editor and return to Scratch.

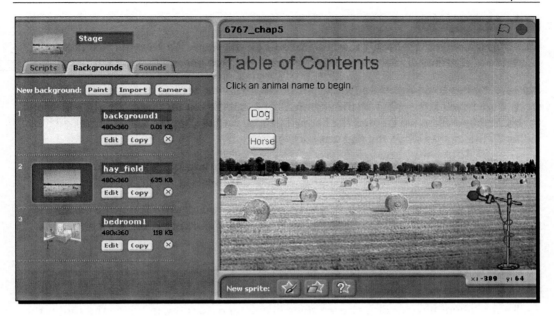

The hay_field background displays with the microphone. Try to move the microphone or make it smaller with the shrink sprite tool. Don't try for too long; you won't be able to manipulate the microphone.

What just happened?

The backgrounds we inserted tell us a story by providing some contextual information. For example, many pet dogs like to spend their days inside on the bed, and while we may not find horses roaming on the hay fields, they do eat hay. It's up to us to use design effectively in our stories.

The microphone provides some unique character to our story that fits with the comedy theme. We added the microphone to the hay field background to form a new image. That's why we can't move the microphone.

Hide that sprite

Click through each stage background to display it on the stage. We have our first problem. The table of contents display on each background, but that doesn't make much sense.

We want sprites to be associated with specific backgrounds, so that each page tells its own story. If we have extra sprites on the screen, they'll muddle our message. We got a first look at this problem when we created the happy birthday card in Chapter 3, and we solved it by hiding all the images when the flag was clicked.

One way we can associate a sprite with a background is by importing a sprite into a background like we did with the microphone in the last excerise.

The trade-off with this approach is that we can no longer manipulate the sprite because it has become integrated with the background. If we look at our sprites list, we'll notice the microphone is not listed.

Time for action – hide the sprites

We'll worry about how we display everything in due time. For now, let's hide the sprites that make up the table of contents:

1. From the sprites list, select the **Table of Contents** sprite.

2. Hide the sprite by double-clicking on the **hide** block in the **Looks** palette.

3. Repeat steps 1 and 2 for each of the remaining sprites: **Dog-TOC**, **Horse-TOC**, and **Instructions**.

Introducing the horse

Our script calls for a horse to be planted in the hay field scene. So, let's add one.

Time for action – import the horse

To start, make sure the hay field is displayed on the stage by clicking on the hay field from your list of stage backgrounds:

1. Add a new sprite by clicking on the **choose new sprite from file** button.

2. Select **horse1-b** from the **Animals** folder and click **OK** to insert the horse.

3. Position the horse next to the microphone by dragging the sprite with your mouse. If the horse and microphone seem out of proportion, resize the **horse** sprite using the shrink or grow tools.

4. A horse standing in front of a microphone begs to be animated, and we're going to begin our animation by adding a second costume. Click on the **Costumes** tab to display the list of costumes.

5. Click the **import** button to open the **Import Costume** dialog box.

6. From the **Animals** folder, select the **horse1-a** image and click **OK**. A second horse image displays in the costumes list, and a preview of the image displays on the stage.

Click on each costume in succession to view how the sprite appears on the stage.

Costumes versus sprites

How we import images into our project determines whether or not we call it a sprite or a costume. You've probably noticed by now that we browse the same files whether we import a costume for a sprite or click on the **choose sprite from file** option. Both are images.

We use a costume to manipulate the appearance of the sprite by switching between the costumes. As a result, we can easily make a sprite run, walk, or dance.

We use a sprite when we want multiple images or characters on the stage at the same time, which we can then control simultaneously.

The horse speaks

We can't expect our horse to stand in front of a microphone and stay silent. Let's give it something to say.

Time for action – the horse talks

Let's write some barnyard humor:

1. From the **Looks** palette, drag the **say Hello for 2 secs** block into the script area.

2. Change the message from **Hello!** to **How do you**.

3. Add another **say Hello for 2 secs** block.

4. Change the message from **Hello!** to **make it rain?**.

 If the sprite is close to the edge of the stage, the speech bubble that displays from the say block may appear at the backend of the sprite.

5. Add a third **say Hello for 2 secs** block.

6. Change the message from **Hello!** to **Mow a hay field**.

7. Change the time from **2** seconds to **1**.

8. Add a **wait 1 secs** block.

9. Change the time from **1** to **3** seconds.

10. Add the **say Hello** block to the script.

11. Change the message from **Hello!** to **Is this thing on?**.

12. Double-click the script to watch our horse tell its first joke.

What just happened?

We wrote a short script to deliver the joke using the say block to display speech bubbles. After three seconds of silence, our horse tossed out a comedic cliché, "Is this thing on?"

We introduced two variations of the say block. For the joke and punchline, the horse spoke for a specified number of seconds. However, at the end of the script, the say block we added did not specify a time value. And if you look at the stage, you'll notice that the speech bubble still displays **Is this thing on?**.

Synchronize the action

If we want the action in our script to continue while the speech bubble displays, we use the say block without a time value. For example, we could make a sprite speak while moving across the stage.

If we use the say block with a time input, the speech bubble displays for the time specified. However, the next block in the script does not execute until the time elapses. This gives us a way to synchronize our scripts.

Time for action – revise the horse talks exercise

Let's revise our script:

1. After the **is this thing on?** block, add a **next costume** block.

2. Add **wait 1 secs**.

3. Add **next costume**.

4. Add a **say** block with an empty message.

5. Double-click on the script to run the code.

What just happened?

It was a tough crowd, and the joke fell flat, causing the horse to nervously rear up on its hind legs. While on its hind legs, the horse spoke, **Is this thing on?**. In our revised script, the speech bubble cleared and created a fluid scene.

Sound

Speech bubbles enable us to convey conversation, even if our conversation is one-sided, but a microphone almost demands sound. In Scratch, we can record or import a sound and then use the Sound palette to replay that sound in our project.

Time for action – a horse whinnies

In this exercise, we'll import a sound from Scratch's library:

1. With the horse sprite selected, click on the **Sounds** tab.

2. Click the **Import** button to display the **Import Sound** dialog box.

3. Browse to the **Animal** folder and select **Horse**.

4. Click **OK** to add the sound to the list of sounds for the horse sprite.

5. Listen to the horse whinny by clicking on the play button.

6. Now, let's add the sound to several places in our script. From the Sound palette, add the **play sound Horse until done** block to the top of the script.

7. Insert a second **play sound Horse until done** block after the **say Mow a hay field for 1 secs** block.

8. Insert the **play sound Horse** block after the **next costume** and before the **wait 1 secs** block.

9. Run the script.

What just happened?

We used Scratch's sound library to add a horse sound to the scene as we continued to build our story. We introduced the horse with a whinny, and then we reiterated the sound after the joke's punchline. Because of what we did with the horse, the first whinny was more of a welcoming message, while the second whinny was a nervous reaction.

I learned how to use some additional markup tools in acrobat!. The first two times we whinnied, we used the **play sound until done** block, so our script stopped until the sound finished playing. At the end, we used the play sound block, which allowed the horse to do several things at one time, such as talk, rear up, and whinny.

We used this combination of actions to make our horse appear nervous, which injected emotion into our story.

Sound formats

Scratch includes a library of sounds that can be used in any of your projects, but you can also easily import your own sounds. The **Import** button on the **Sounds** tab provides a dialog box that lets you browse the Scratch sounds on your own computer.

In addition to the MP3 format, Scratch can play uncompressed WAV, AU, and AIF sound files in 8-bit or 16-bit sample rates.

The dog enters

With our horse scene complete, we'll move on to the dog.

Time for action – bring out the dog

Let's prepare the stage by hiding the horse and displaying the bedroom background. We're going to keep an element of consistency in our story and add the microphone to the dog's scene:

1. Edit the bedroom background to open it in the Paint Editor

2. Import the microphone into the background like we did when we imported the microphone into the hay_field.

3. Position the microphone in the lower-left corner of the stage, and make it smaller by clicking on the Shrink button twice.

4. The microphone points off stage, so flip it horizontally.

5. Click **OK** to save the changes and exit the Paint Editor.

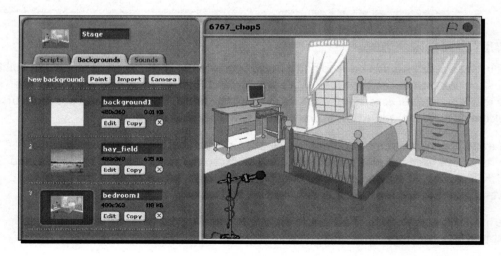

6. Next, add the main character for this screen, the dog. Click on the **choose new sprite from file** button.

7. In the **Animals** folder, find **dog2-a**, the blue dog with a raised eyebrow, and select it. Click **OK** to add it to the stage. Flip it horizontally if it faces away from the microphone.

8. Click **OK** to exit the Paint Editor.

9. Position the dog so that it is talking into the microphone.

X and Y coordinates mark the spot

In Chapter 3, we learned that each spot on the stage can be precisely identified by its coordinates. Let's see where on the grid our dog stands.

Time for action – stay dog

In this exercise, we're going to start the scene by positioning the dog in front of the microphone and end the scene by lying the dog on its side.

1. Find the dog's current X and Y coordinates by looking in the Sprite Info section. Just above the **Scripts**, **Costumes**, and **Sounds** tabs, the sprite's current location displays.

2. From the Motion palette, drag the **set x to 0** block to the scripts area. Change the input value to the dog's X value. My example uses **-56**.

3. Add the **set y to 0** block.

4. Change the input value to the dog's Y value. My example uses **-116**.

5. Let's identify some coordinates in front of the dresser. As you move your mouse around the stage, Scratch tracks the X and Y position of the mouse. The information is displayed as **x** and **y** values in the space between the stage and the sprites list.

6. From the Motion palette, add the **glide 1 secs to x: -56 y: -116** block to the scripts area, but do not attach it to the previous blocks.

 Note that the **glide** block is populated with the current x and y coordinates of the selected sprite.

7. Change the **x** value on the **glide** block to **152**.

8. Change the **y** value on the **glide** block to **-47**.

9. Change the **secs** value on the **glide** block to **2**.

 The more seconds you add, the longer it takes the dog to reach its coordinates.

10. Run each script by double-clicking on it and observe how the dog changes its positions.

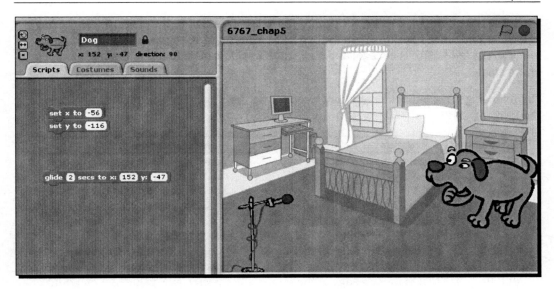

What just happened?

We issued a series of commands, and our dog responded with precision. The first command sets the dog's X and Y position next to the microphone. The second command moves the dog to the new X and Y coordinates in front of the dresser. The 2 seconds we specified in the glide block means the dog takes 2 seconds to reach the new coordinates. If we wanted the sprite to amble along, we could set a higher value, such as 10 seconds.

When we built the horse scene, we didn't need to know the position of the horse because it didn't move. Each time we displayed the horse, it was in the same location.

However, the dog changes position as the scene plays out, and since Scratch remembers the sprite's previous position, we need to ensure that the dog always starts in front of the microphone when the scene starts.

Position on the grid

The X axis divides the stage into equal halves horizontally, and the Y axis divides the stage into equal halves vertically. The two axes intersect in the middle of the screen or at coordinates (0,0).

If a sprite has a positive X value, it's positioned in the right half of the stage. If a sprite has a positive Y value, it's positioned in the top half of the stage. A negative X value can be found in the left half of the stage, and a negative Y value can be found in the bottom half of the stage.

The following table defines several key locations on the stage. The coordinates are listed in the format (X,Y):

Coordinate	Description	More Information
(0,0)	Marks the center of the stage.	To set a sprite in the middle of the stage horizontally, specify X:0. To set a sprite in the middle vertically, specify Y:0.
(240,0)	Marks right edge of the stage.	Specify a Y value to move up or down the right edge.
(-240,0)	Marks the left edge of the stage.	Specify a Y value to move up or down the left edge.
(0,180)	Marks the top edge of the stage.	Specify an X value to move right or left across the top edge.
(0,-180)	Marks the bottom edge of the stage.	Specify an X value to move right or left across the bottom edge.

The following screenshot shows the Scratch stage with an (X,Y) grid as a background. This grid is one of Scratch's included backgrounds.

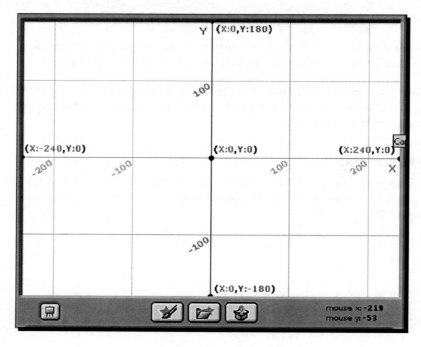

Pop quiz

1. What is the significance of the say for block?
   - ◆ You can specify how long the speech bubble displays.
   - ◆ The script stops for the time specified.
   - ◆ All of the above.

2. What point on the Scratch stage do the coordinates -240,-180 represent?
   - ◆ Center stage.
   - ◆ Bottom-left of the stage.
   - ◆ Top-right of the stage.

Pointed in the right direction

Most dogs don't walk across the room backwards like ours does. Let's get our dog to walk forward.

Time for action – turn to the left

Using the Motion palette, turn the dog around:

1. Add the **point in direction 90** block to the top of the **glide** block.
2. Change **90** to **-90**.
3. Add the **point in direction 90** block to the top of the **set x to -56** block.
4. Double-click each script to run the blocks of code. The dog now faces in the correct direction, but it rotates upside down.
5. Remember in Chapter 3 when we discovered the flip rotation button? Use the rotation buttons so that the dog only faces left-right.

What just happened?

If you thought about the blocks of code we just added, you might be wondering why we set the direction to -90 to make our sprite face right and glide away from the microphone.

Remember, we altered the dog's costume when we added it. The dog's face pointed to the right by default, but we flipped it horizontally. Now, the dog's tail points to the right. Scratch didn't identify the sprite in terms of the dog's face and the dog's tail. Instead, it saw the left side of the sprite and the right side of the sprite.

When we returned the dog to the front of the microphone, we pointed the sprite's direction to 90 to make the dog face the microphone.

Degrees of direction

Scratch enables us to point a sprite in one of the four major directions by default: 90 (right), -90 (left), 180 (down), and 0 (up).

To enter a non-default direction, click in the input box of the **point in direction** block, and type the new value. The following help window from Scratch illustrates how to use the **point in direction** block:

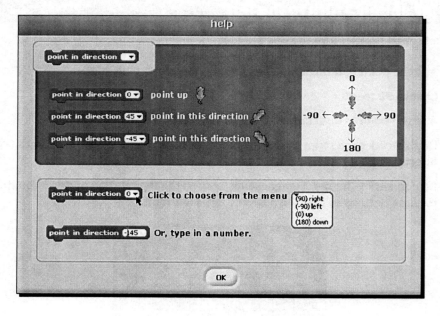

 You can view the help topic for any block by right-clicking on the block and selecting **Help**.

Sound effects

Importing sounds into our project makes adding sound effects easy, but the musically inclined among us will appreciate the ability to build custom sound effects. Let's try our hand at creating a drum effect that plays on the punchline of the dog's joke.

Time for action – hit the cymbals

Our script will be relatively simple. We'll strike a drum, and we'll follow that with cymbals:

1. Drag the **play drum 48 for 0.2 beats** block to the script area, but do not attach it to the existing scripts. Change the **48** to **(40) Electric Snare**.

2. Snap a second **play drum 48 for 0.2 beats** block to the previous **play drum** block. Change the **48** to **(57) Crash Cymbal 2**. Set the beats value to **0.4**.

3. Add a third **play drum 48 for 0.2 beats** block. Change the **48** to **(38) Acoustic Snare**. Set the beats value to **0.1**.

4. Add a **set tempo to 60 bpm** block to the top of the sound script.

5. Change **60** to **120**.

6. Snap the **rest for 0.2 beats** block in place between the two play drum blocks.

7. Double-click the **sound** blocks to hear the effect.

Feel free to tweak the values and experiment with the sound.

What just happened?

Our dog's jokes might not be as good as the horse's, so we have added some drums to punctuate the punchline. Now our audience will know when to laugh.

By arranging three drum effects, tempo, and rest, we've created a familiar *da dat chsh* drum roll. If we wanted a faster pace to our sound, we would use a higher tempo.

Select an instrument

Scratch includes 46 types of drums as options in the **play drum** block. When you click on the drum effect drop-down list, you can page through the options by clicking on the **more...** link at the bottom. See the following screenshot:

What if you don't want to play a drum? Scratch includes 128 instruments. Let's take a look.

Time for action – applause, please

Everyone appreciates applause. Let's use Scratch's instruments to add some new effects to our story:

1. From the Sound palette, drag a **set tempo to 60 bpm** block to the scripts area, but do not attach it to any of the previous scripts. Add a **set instrument to 1** block after the tempo block.

2. Change the instrument value to 127 applause. Click the **more...** option until value **127** displays.

3. Double-click the block to play the sound. You should hear silence.

4. Add the **play note 60 for 0.5 beats** block to the script.

5. Change the beats value from **0.5** to **1**.

6. From the Control palette, drag a **repeat 10** block to the scripts area and wrap it around the three sound blocks we just added.

7. Double-click the blocks and listen to the applause.

Our applause needs some work. Actually, I'll be honest with you. It sounds horrible. You'll get a chance to fix it soon.

What just happened?

We used the term instrument liberally. Even though we could have chosen standard musical instruments such as organs, guitars, and pianos, our story called for an applause.

Selecting an instrument by itself did not produce any sound the way the **play drum** block did. In order to get sound, we had to first select a musical note, so we chose to play our applause in C for one beat.

The **repeat** block gave us the sense of roaring applause that would not be possible if we chose to play only one beat of applause.

Play a note

When we click on the note value in the **play note** block, a keyboard displays. As you hover your mouse over the key, the note and its associated number display.

If you want a higher-pitched note, select a higher number in the **play note** block.

Have a go hero

The applause we added doesn't sound good because it's choppy. You can experiment and try to make the applause smoother.

Or, you can turn to the Internet to find an applause sound effect and play it with the **play sound until done** block instead of repeating the tempo, notes, and instruments we added in the exercise.

Pop quiz

1. If you specify a value of 90 in the point in direction block, what position does that represent on the Scratch stage?

   ◆ Up
   ◆ Down
   ◆ Left
   ◆ Right

2. In order to play an instrument you need to accompany the set instrument to block with a:

   ◆ play sound until done block
   ◆ play drum block
   ◆ play note block

Piece the dog scene together

Right now, our scene has four disconnected sets of blocks. There's nothing wrong with that. Our projects do not always unfold in a linear pattern.

It's time to write the joke. You should be able to build the joke sequence without much help from me. Here is the joke: "What are the top three reasons dogs don't use computers?" The responses:

◆ Sit and stay were hard enough—grep and awk are out of the question!
◆ They can't stop hunting the mouse.
◆ Carpal Paw Syndrome!

Most of you will be wondering what grep and awk are. Let's just say our dog caters to a Linux-friendly audience. Feel free to change the joke to incorporate your favorite operating system, as you see fit.

Add a one second pause between each line. If you need some help, the screenshot below shows a possible approach:

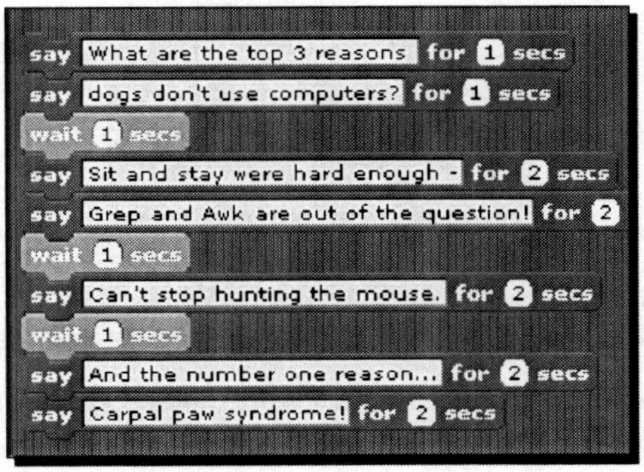

In the next exercise, we'll refer to this block of code as the joke sequence.

Time for action – joke, please

With jokes in hand, let's integrate them into our scene:

1. Snap the joke sequence to the bottom of the **set y to -116** block.

2. Snap the **point in direction -90** and **glide 2 secs to x: 152 y: -47** blocks to the bottom of the joke sequence. Check your work against the following screenshot.

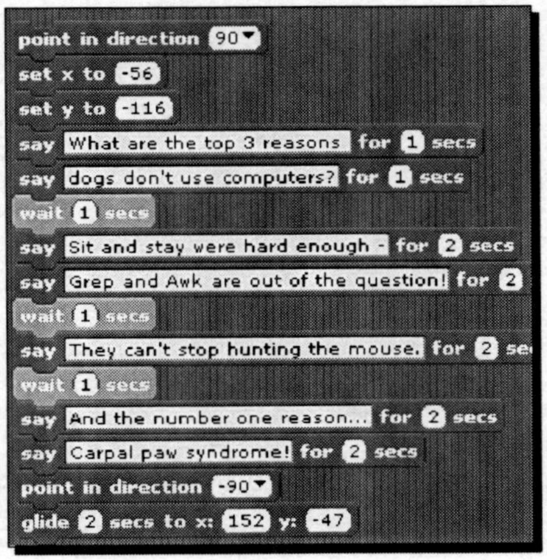

3. Snap the applause script to the bottom of the **glide 2 secs to x: 152 y: -47** block.

 If you need more space to work with in the scripts area, you can use the "switch to small stage" mode by clicking the small stage button located above the flag and stop sign buttons.

4. Now, let's add our drum effect to the script. We have three jokes, so we will use a broadcast and wait block to play the drum effects after each joke.

5. After each joke, insert a **broadcast and wait** block. Create and select a new broadcast message for each **broadcast** block: **play drums**.

6. Add a **when I receive** block to the top of the drum effects and select the **play drums** message.

7. Double-click the script to watch the scene unfold.

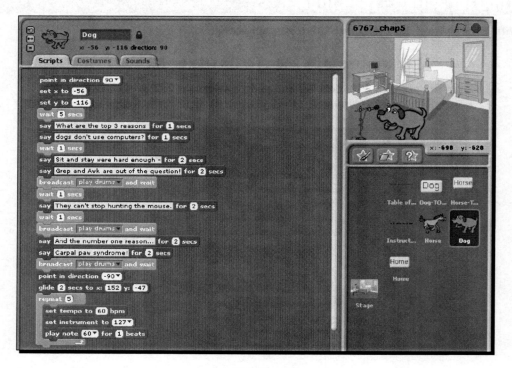

What just happened?

The joke was a roaring success, and the crowd loved it. We punctuated the punchline with a drum. In order to make our scene work, we had to connect the several individual snippets of blocks we've been building for the dog scene.

The **broadcast and wait** block lets us synchronize the action. After each joke, we crashed the cymbals, but our script waited until the cymbals finished playing before it proceeded to the next line.

At the conclusion of the scene, our dog left to roaring applause.

Have a go hero

There's only one problem with our sprite. The dog wanders off stage after telling the joke, but its expression never changes. Give the dog a different expression, and make him lie down on his side.

See the following screenshot for a hint:

Control the story

The only step left is to add some controls to the project so our users can click from one scene to the next. For navigation, we want to give users the ability to click on an item from the table of contents to play the scene. The user can then click back to the table of contents by clicking on a home link.

Time for action – hide TOC

Before we begin, hide the dog by double-clicking the **hide** block from the **Looks** palette.

1. Let's get back to the plain white background. With the stage selected, click on the **Backgrounds** tab. Select background 1.

2. Display the **Table of Contents, Dog-TOC, Horse-TOC,** and **Instructions** sprites by right-clicking on each one from the sprites list and selecting **show**.

3. Let's make the **Dog-TOC** sprite clickable. From the sprites list, select the **Dog-TOC** sprite.

4. From the **Control** palette, drag the **when Dog-TOC clicked** block into the scripts area.

5. Add a **broadcast** block to the script and create a new broadcast message: **enter dog**.

6. When we click the **Dog-TOC** sprite, we want all visible sprites to hide. Select the **Table of Contents** sprite from the sprites list.

7. From the **Control** palette, add the **when I receive enter dog** block to the scripts area.

8. From the **Looks** palette, add the **hide** block to the script.

What just happened?

Before we can play our scene, we need to clear the stage. We do that with the broadcast message that gets sent when we click on Dog from the table of contents.

From our previous projects, we learned that all sprites receive a broadcast message, but they do not act on the message unless told to do so. The exercise built those instructions, and if we were to click the **Home** button right now, only the words "Table of Contents" would disappear.

Your hero task is to make all of the other visible sprites hide.

Have a go hero

Finish the task. Hide the remaining table of contents items: **Horse-TOC**, **Instructions**, and **Tables of Contents**.

Time for action – enter dog

We continue to build around the broadcast message **enter dog**. This time we need to display the sprites:

1. Now that we have cleared the table of contents, we need to load the dog scene. We'll bring in the background first and the dog second.

2. With the stage selected, click on the **Scripts** tab.

3. From the **Control** palette, add the **when I receive enter dog** block to the scripts area.

4. From the **Looks** palette, add the **switch to background** block to the script and choose **bedroom1**.

5. Click on the **dog** sprite to display the scripts area for the dog.

6. From the **Control** palette, drag the **when I receive enter dog** block to the scripts area and attach it to the top of the existing script.

7. From the **Looks** palette, snap the **show** block in place after the **when I receive enter dog** block.

8. After the scene changes, we want to delay the start of the action for a few seconds so that our users have a chance to acclimate to the switch. Snap a **wait 1 secs** block in place after the **set y to -116** block and change the input value to **5**.

9. Click on the **Dog** button from the table of contents and watch the dog scene load and play.

What just happened?

With one mouse click, we loaded our wise-cracking dog and learned why dogs don't use computers. We used the **broadcast** block to coordinate the sequence of our scene. Not only did the broadcast message **enter dog** hide the table of contents page, but it also loaded the dog scene.

We needed to add some timing to control the scene by delaying the start of the joke by five seconds. Without the delay, everything happened at one time: the background displayed, the dog displayed, and the joke started. It was too abrupt.

Time for action – exit dog

After a scene plays out, we need to give our users a way to play the next scene. We're going to return to the table of contents and allow the user to select the next item. Let's add the controls:

1. Using the Paint Editor, create a new button with the text **Home** written on it and position it on the top-left of the stage.

2. Manually display the **Home** button by selecting the **Home** sprite that you just created from the sprites list. Right-click on the sprite and select **show**.

3. From the **Control** palette, drag the **when clicked** block into the scripts area and select **Home** from the drop-down list.

4. Add a **broadcast** block to the script. Create the following broadcast message: **Show TOC**.

5. Clear the **Home** sprite from the stage by adding the **hide** block from the **Looks** palette.

What just happened?

As we develop the project, we continue to refine how it works. This time, we created a **Home** button that cleared the dog scene based on a broadcast message.

Have a go hero

Finish the task. Hide the **dog** sprite and bedroom background based on the **Show TOC** broadcast message.

Time for action – show TOC

Next, we will programmatically show the table of contents.

1. Select the **Dog-TOC** sprite from the sprites list.

2. From the **Control** palette, drag the **when I receive enter dog** block to the scripts area and select **show TOC**.

3. From the **Looks** palette, add the **show** block to the script.

4. Double-click on the script to make the **Dog-TOC** sprite appear. The only item on the stage will be the **Dog** button.

5. Click the **Dog** menu to play the dog scene.

6. Now click on the **Home** button. Oops! We forgot a script. Let's add a **Control** block to display the **Home** button when we click on **Dog** in the table of contents.

7. From the sprites list, select **Home**.

8. From the **Control** palette, add the **when I receive enter dog** block to the scripts area.

9. From the **Looks** palette, add the **show** block.

10. Double-click the script to display the **Home** sprite.

You can play the scene over and over again by alternatively clicking on the **Dog** and **Home** buttons.

What just happened?

We completed the work to let the user flip between the table of contents and a chapter in the book. The concept was straightforward. We displayed and hid sprites based on what the user clicked.

Have a go hero

Finish the task. Display the remainder of the sprites on the table of contents when the user clicks the **Home** button.

Build sequence

Whether we guide the user through the project or make it interactive, we need to think about the question, "What happens when ... ?" The answer to this question becomes the basis for how we move our users through the project.

In Chapter 4, we built projects that progressed through a series of steps. In essence, we started with an action and just kept adding to it. The user didn't have to be involved.

In this chapter, we created a project that allowed the user to choose a path.

Have a go hero

The horse deserves to tell its joke, too. Create the sequences to hide and display the horse scene.

Next steps

There seems to be a near infinite number of ways in which you can adapt this project. You could create a chapbook to share your poems, or you could create a book for your child that teaches them their ABCs. Do you want to make the scenes more dynamic and action-filled? Add multiple actors to a single screen and have them carry on a conversation.

Mix in music that plays during the transitions, or narrate your own story using the built-in record function.

Summary

What an exciting chapter! Programming in Scratch is easy; it's telling a story that's hard. Let's take a breath and recapitulate what we've learned.

In this chapter, we focused on telling a story, and everything we did added context to the story, including the way we animated our sprites with costumes. Not only do we need to think about how each scene unfolded, but we also need to provide navigation from one scene to the next.

Our sprites spoke for the first time in this chapter using speech bubbles. We learned how to apply the different types of **say** blocks to affect how our sprites spoke.

We enhanced our scripts with sound effects, including drums and musical instruments. We explored tempo and musical notes as ways to modify a sound. We also saw how easy it was to import our own sounds and use them with the project.

In our dog scene, the sprite moved around the screen, so we learned how to set the position of the dog using the X and Y coordinates.

We wrapped up all this activity with some control mechanisms and gave each sprite explicit instructions based on what the user selected on the screen. This control was interesting because we made a single broadcast message to control many sprites, and depending on the sprite, each behaved differently.

In the next chapter, we'll continue to explore motion as we remix the classic arcade game Pong.

6
Arcade Games

This chapter presents a new challenge for us because we're starting with somebody else's work. This means we'll have to spend some time figuring out what the existing code does before we can make our customizations and build a new game.

In this chapter, we will:

- *Analyze and customize an existing Scratch project to create something new*
- *Define and interpret variables to evaluate dynamic data*
- *Control the actions of the sprites based on conditional information*

Let's create our version of the classic arcade game Pong.

Troll pong

Let's flash back to 1972 and create a clone of the popular Atari video game Pong. Instead of starting this program from scratch, we're going to start with a sample project that we can use as a basis for our creativity.

Time for action – open the sample pong project

Open the sample pong game that's included with Scratch:

1. In Scratch, click the **File | Open** menu to display the **Open Project** dialog box.

2. Click on the Examples button. Then open the **Games** folder and select **Pong**. Click **OK** to load the project.

3. Play the game by clicking on the flag. Move the mouse left or right to control the paddle and hit the ball.

4. Move the mouse up and down the stage. The paddle doesn't move.

5. When you've had enough, stop the game.

6. Let's get some more information about what the ball is doing. From the **Motion** palette, click on the checkbox next to **direction**. This displays a new report block on the stage that shows the ball's direction.

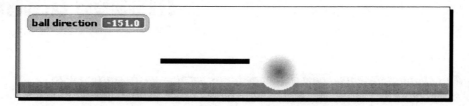

7. Play the game again and note how the ball direction value changes as the ball travels across the stage. When you're done, let the ball hit the red stripe.

8. Let's take a look at the paddle's script by clicking on the **paddle** from the sprites list.

9. We can also monitor the paddle's x coordinate as you move it across the stage. From the **Motion** palette, click the checkbox next to the **x position** block. A new block displays on the stage that reports the paddle's current x position.

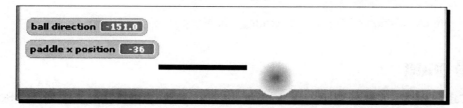

10. Now, let's take a look at scripts that are associated with the ball by selecting the **ball** from the sprites list. See the following screenshot:

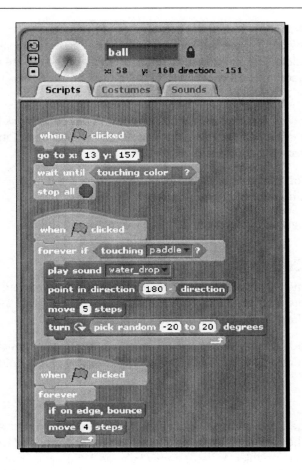

11. Play another game. Watch the monitor blocks report the direction of the ball and the location of the paddle in real time.

What just happened?

If real table tennis was this easy, I might enjoy it more! Let's analyze our project from the time we clicked the flag.

The mission was simple: Keep the ball from landing on the red stripe to keep the game alive. As we noted, our game is fairly simple. We have a paddle and a ball. The paddle moves are based on our mouse's actions. As we drag the mouse to the left, so went the paddle. However, the paddle didn't respond to up and down mouse movements.

We tracked the ball's direction and the paddle's x coordinate by enabling the **direction** and **x position** blocks, respectively. Clicking on the checkbox next to each block placed a real-time readout of the block's value on the stage.

In Chapter 5, we learned how to find the coordinates of the mouse via the mouse x and mouse y values. In the pong game, we learned how to use the mouse x value to control the movement of the paddle. The script reads the x coordinate of the mouse and sets it to the x coordinate of the paddle. The x coordinate of the mouse became the x coordinate of the **paddle** sprite.

The direction change was accomplished with the **point in direction** block that executed when the ball touched the paddle. The script calculated the new direction by subtracting the ball's direction from the constant value of 180.

As the ball bounced off the paddle, the script put a twist on the direction change by turning the ball by a random number of degrees between -20 and 20.

We'll look at the project scripts in more detail as we customize them.

Dynamic interaction

The **mouse x** and **mouse y** blocks enable us to use the X and Y coordinates of the mouse as direct input values into a script. We can use the values to move a sprite around the stage or change a graphical effect based on the mouse x or mouse y values.

Since the mouse x and mouse y values are numeric, we can use them as the input for any block that accepts a numeric value. The **mouse x** and **mouse y** blocks hold variable data.

Variables

Variables store numbers and information. Let's think of a variable you probably care very deeply about: your checking account balance. Each time you deposit or withdraw money, the balance changes, and the bank calculates a new balance. When you want to know how much money you have available, you log in to your online bank account and check the balance.

We use variables to store values that can change as our program runs. The value assigned to a variable is often the output of a previous programming command or calculation that we use as an input for a future calculation.

Consider our bank account. The bank outputs our balance. When we review the family budget, we take the bank balance into consideration as we pay our bills and make various decisions based on the budget needs and bank balance.

Variables generally make our programming life easier, whereas constant values give us less flexibility and can complicate our code. The value of a constant never changes. If we want to change a calculation that uses a constant, we have to go into the scripts, find the value, and change it. The numbers in your scripts, such as 10 or the year of your birthday, represent constant values.

We'll work more with variable data in the upcoming chapters. Let's get back to pong.

Time for action – change direction

Let's calculate a new direction:

1. Select the **ball** sprite from the sprites list, and find the script that contains the **point in direction** block. See the following screenshot:

2. Change the calculation used to redirect the ball. Change **180** to **90**.

3. Click the flag to test. Observe the results.

4. Let's simplify the direction change. Drag the green number block that currently contains the calculation **90 – direction** out of the **point in direction** block. You can drag it down to a blank spot in the scripts area.

5. Change the value of the **point in direction** block to **180**. Click the flag to play. Observe the results. The ball should always fall through the paddle and to the bottom of the screen.

6. Change the value of the **point in direction** block to **0**. Click the flag to play. This time the ball bounces back up when it hits the paddle.

What just happened?

We definitely had some variations in our game. Using **90 – direction** did not produce a playable game. When we simplified the direction to **180**, our game exhibited a similar unplayable behavior, but a setting of **0** seemed to work.

In the original **point in direction** block calculation, 180 is a constant and we subtracted the direction of the ball, which was stored in the **direction** block, a variable, to get a new direction value.

Here's an example calculation that uses 121 as the ball's direction. The program subtracts 121 from 180 to get 59. Therefore, the value of the **point in direction** block becomes 59.

The original calculation always seems to bounce the ball off the paddle and put it in play. When we changed our calculation to use **90 – direction**, the ball's behavior became much more erratic, and it may have failed to bounce off the paddle.

When we simplified our direction, we tried setting a constant value of 180, but if you recall our direction discussion from Chapter 5, you will remember that 180 represented a down direction. When we set the direction to 0, the ball bounced off the paddle as expected.

The **point in direction** block is not the only calculation in the script that affects the ball's direction. Let's take a closer look.

Time for action – remove the random turn

We're going to remove the block that tells the ball to turn a random number of degrees and see what happens:

1. Drag the **turn clockwise degrees** block to a blank spot in the scripts area so that it doesn't run when we play the game.

2. Click on the flag. Each time the ball hits the paddle, it bounces straight up. Your script should look like the following screenshot:

What just happened?

You didn't need any skill or coordination in this game, as long as you hit the ball the first time. The trajectory of the ball never changed; it went straight up and came straight back down.

I made a sandwich while the ball bounced off the paddle. That's not exactly fun.

The **point in direction** block and the **turn clockwise degrees** block that calculates a random value between -20 and 20 work together to affect how the ball bounces off the paddle.

Have a go hero

Get the script back to its original state. Add the number block **180 – direction** back to the input value of the **point in direction** block. Add the **random turn** block back to the script.

Experiment with and select new directions, if you wish.

Customize the sprites

The first real change we want to make to the pong project is to add a new ball. We will also change the appearance of the paddle. However, we want to make sure we keep the original scripts in place. Let's take a look.

Time for action – beach ball pong

Let's replace the colored circle with a beach ball:

1. Click on the **Costumes** tab of the **ball** sprite.

2. Add a new costume by clicking on the **Import** button.

3. In the **Import Costume** dialog box, open the **Things** folder. Select the **beachball1** and click **OK** to add it as a costume for the **ball**.

4. Delete **costume1**, the blue gradient, by clicking on the **x** for costume1.

5. Click the flag to play the game. Now, we're playing with a colorful beach ball, but it's a bit big.

6. Use the shrink sprite tool to make the **ball** sprite smaller. Make it as small as you want.

7. From the **Looks** palette, add the **change color effect by 25** block to the **forever if touching paddle** block.

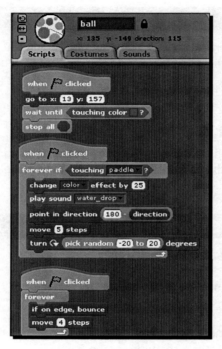

What just happened?

We took the first step toward infusing this project with our own colorful character. Did you note the trick we used to change our ball while keeping the original scripts?

If we had first deleted the **ball** sprite, we would have lost all the scripts. By adding the beach ball as a costume, the original blue circle became just a costume for the **ball** sprite. We deleted the blue circle, and voila!—the appearance of the sprite changed to the beach ball.

Have a go hero

Change the **paddle** sprite to a person, troll, or some other character. You may need to resize your sprite and manually position it at the bottom of the stage.

Time for action – add new paddle controls

Moving the paddle with the mouse works, but users on a laptop may find the trackpad a bit difficult to use. We're going to use the left and right arrow keys for our movement:

1. Select the **paddle** sprite from the sprites list.

2. From the **Control** palette, add **when space key pressed** to the scripts area.

3. Change the value to **left arrow**.

4. From the **Motion** palette, add the **move 10 steps** block to the **when left arrow key pressed** block.

5. Change the value to **-10** steps.

6. Add a second control block that uses the right arrow key to move 10 steps.

7. Play the game and use the arrow keys to move.

8. Let's try to take bigger steps. Change the number of steps to a larger number, such as **50**.

9. Clean up the script by removing the original **when flag clicked** block that used the mouse x value to control the sprite. We no longer need it.

10. From the **Motion** palette, uncheck the **x position** block.

What just happened?

The complexion of our game has changed. If you did the hero exercise, your **paddle** sprite probably has a smaller surface to hit the ball than the original paddle. The arrow keys restrict how fast the sprite moves across the stage.

Each time we pressed the key, the sprite stepped to the left or right depending on which arrow we used. The **move 50 steps** block moved five times as far with one keystroke than the **move 10 steps** block.

Play theme music, forever

A video game just wouldn't be any fun without some music, but before we can add music, we need to find some. You can use an MP3 from your music collection, search Creative Commons, or use a site such as `free-loops.com`. If you're musically inclined, you could build your music loop using the sounds we learned about in Chapter 5.

If you don't have a favorite sound, don't worry. Scratch includes a library of sounds you can use.

Time for action – add background music

Let's add some music:

1. From the sprites list, select **Stage**.

2. Add the **when flag clicked** block to the stage's script area.

3. From the **Control** palette, add the **forever** block.

4. From the **Sounds** palette, add the **play sound until done** block to the **forever** block.

5. Let's import the music file. Click on the **Sounds** tab, and then click the **Import** button to display the **Import Sound** dialog box.

6. Browse to and select the music file you want to add. For example, I'm going to use the Drum sound from the **Music Loops** folder in Scratch's sound library. Click **OK** to add the new sound.

7. Click back to the **Scripts** tab and set the **play sound** block to use the new sound file.

8. Click the **flag** to play the game and listen to the music.

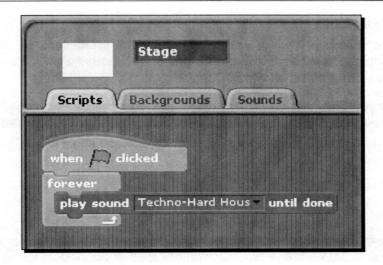

What just happened?

Hopefully, you chose a sound or song you liked. Each time we clicked the flag, the music played forever—or as long as the ball did not hit the red stripe. It was otherwise independent of the ball or the paddle, which is why we associated the script with the stage.

If your music didn't play based on the exercise, make sure you added the script to the stage, not the **paddle** or **ball** sprites.

Do something, forever

When we want to iterate through a script an infinite number of times, we can use a **forever** block. Sound is only one example. Another example includes moving across the stage while switching between costumes, which can be included in a forever loop to give the appearance of walking or running. You could also apply a graphical effect to a sprite every five seconds.

The length of time it takes to complete one trip through the loop depends on the code that's included in the loop. For example, if we play a seven minute song, the loop repeats once every seven minutes.

The forever loops can be as complicated as we need them to be. We can nest other forever loops, **repeat** blocks, and multi-block scripts.

Working with sound

We've now seen two ways in which we can work with sound. In Chapter 5, we added sound effects to play based on an event. In Chapter 6, we imported a music file that plays continuously as theme music.

Have a go hero

Find a sound that might be suitable for a *game over* sound, and play it when the ball hits the red stripe.

[Hint: Wait until the ball touches the red color.]

Pop quiz

Which of the following resources can you use to import a sound into your project?

- ◆ Scratch's built-in sound library
- ◆ Your personal MP3 collection
- ◆ A third-party sound download site
- ◆ All of the above

Forever, on one condition

We've already seen a few instances of a forever loop, and we know that the code inside the forever loop runs as long as the project runs. Adding the background music to the game is an example. Click the flag, and the music stops. If the ball hits the red stripe, the entire game stops.

Sometimes, we may want to run a block of code only when a certain condition is met. Let's take a look at a conditional loop using the **forever if** block.

Time for action – paddle meets ball

When the ball contacts the paddle, let's make our paddle say, "Nice Shot!"

1. Select the **paddle** sprite.
2. Add a **when flag clicked** block from the **Control** palette.
3. From the **Control** palette, add a **forever if** block.

4.   From the **Looks** palette, add a **say for 2 secs** block to the **forever if** block.

5.   Change **Hello!** to something fun, like **Nice shot!** Change **2** seconds to **1** second so our message doesn't display too long.

6.   From the **Sensing** palette, drag the **touching** block into the input value of the **forever if** block.

7.   From the drop-down list in the **touching** block, select **ball**.

8.   Click the flag to play the game.

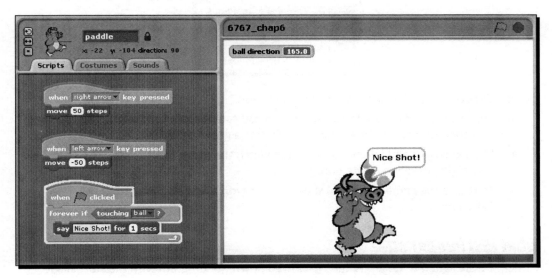

What just happened?

Hey, that was a nice shot! Did you think our paddle was a bit pompous to dish out the self-compliment each time the ball and paddle collided?

As long as the ball stays in play, the paddle repeats its message after each shot because we added the **forever if touching ball** block. Our keyword was **if**.

Let's slow down our program and take a closer look.

Start single stepping

Scratch includes a start single stepping setting that significantly slows down the program and allows us to see the code as the program runs. Let's use the start single stepping option to examine our **forever if** block.

1. From the **Edit** menu, select the **start single stepping** option.

2. Click the flag. The game starts in slow motion.
3. Select the **paddle** from the sprites list so you can observe the scripts. The **touching ball** condition on the **forever if** block flashes a green color.
4. Press the right and left arrow keys, and watch the **move** blocks flash. The scripts are also highlighted in a white border.
5. To return the game to normal speed, select **stop single stepping** from the **Extras** menu.

What just happened?

Scratch was designed to teach. When we slowed down the program with the start single stepping option, we told Scratch to show us each step of the script as it executes. We were able to see each step of our program, block by block.

The **forever if** block made the script constantly check if the paddle was touching the ball. Only when the two sprites touched did the **say Nice Shot! for 1 secs** block flash.

If we were to replace the **forever if touching ball** block with an **if touching ball**, the script would make only one check when we clicked the green flag. Go ahead and give it a try. I'll wait.

Conditional statements

Conditional statements are an integral part of our everyday, non-programming thought process in that we evaluate our environmental inputs and take actions based on the results. Here's an example: You want to cross the street. If there are no oncoming cars, you cross the street. If there are oncoming cars, you wait and check again.

If we reframe our example of crossing the street into a programming statement using one of Scratch's conditional statements, we might say the following:

1. If there are no cars coming, cross the street.
2. If there are cars coming, do not cross the street; or else, cross the street.
3. You'll wait until there are no cars coming, and then cross the street.
4. When you receive a walk signal, cross the street.

The conditional blocks control when and if something happens, so we find them in the **Control** palette.

Pop quiz

1. To analyze the project's script one block at a time, you would use which of the following features?
   - Block-by-block analyzer
   - Single stepping
   - Watch the Scratch scripts really carefully

2. Which of the following blocks represent a conditional statement?
   - Move 10 steps
   - Forever
   - Forever if
   - Repeat 10

What's the score?

How do we know how good we are if our game doesn't keep score? The next step in our project is to add points to our score each time we hit the ball and to display the value on the stage.

Before we begin, turn off any remaining monitors from the stage because we no longer need them.

Time for action – add a score variable

To keep score we need to set up a variable and add a condition to increment the score when the ball touches the paddle:

1. From the **Variables** palette, click on the **Make a variable** button to display the **Variable name** dialog box.

2. Type the word **Score** and select the **For all sprites** option.

3. Click **OK** to add the variable. The **Variables** palette displays several new blocks and the **Score** reporter block automatically displays on the stage.

4. We will calculate the score based on the ball's behavior, so select the **ball** from the list of sprites.

5. Add **change Score by 1** to the inside of the **forever if touching paddle** block.

6. Click the flag and play the game. Each time the two sprites collide, the score increments. Play the game several times, and note that we have a running score.

7. Let's reset the score to **0**. From the **Variables** palette, add the **set Score to 0** block between the **when flag clicked** and **forever if touching paddle** blocks.

8. Play the game a few times. The score resets to 0, each time you click the green flag.

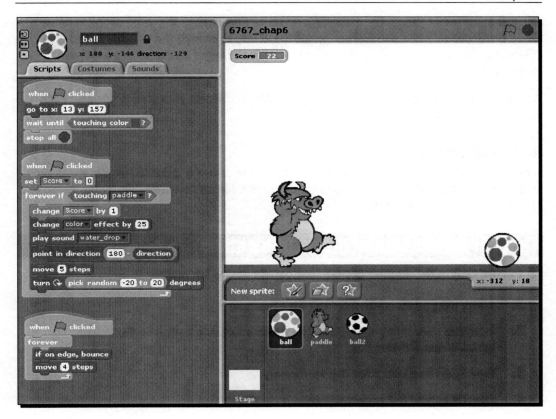

What just happened?

Each time the ball touched the paddle, we added a point to the Score variable and reported it on the stage for all to see. At the start of each game, we reset the score to 0 so the player doesn't add to the score from the previous game.

For all sprites

When we make a variable for a sprite, we can select the **For all sprites** option. This makes a global variable, which means that all our sprites can access the value stored in the variable.

This has many implications. For example, one sprite may change the value of the variable based on an event, while another sprite has the ability to change the variable based on a different event. We can also use the variable's value to trigger an event for an individual sprite, such as a message broadcast.

Working with too many global variables will quickly complicate your scripts because each sprite has access to the variable.

For this sprite only

In contrast to the global variable, Scratch enables us to create a variable **For this sprite only**. Programmers often call this a local variable because it can be accessed only by the sprite you assigned it to. Let's take a look.

Time for action – count the paddle's steps

For fun, let's count the number of times our paddle moves left and right:

1. Select the **paddle** sprite from the list of sprites.

2. From the **Variables** palette, click the **Make a variable** button to display the **Variable name** dialog box.

3. Type **Steps** and select **For this sprite only**.

4. Click **OK** to add the variable.

5. Click on the **ball** sprite and review the blocks available in the Variables palette. **Steps** is not an option. Select the **paddle** sprite again.

6. From the **Variables** palette, add the **change by 1** block to the end of each of the scripts that move the paddle with the left and right arrow key.

7. Change the value from **Score** to **Steps**. Change the value from **1** to **50** in each script.

8. From the **Variables** palette, add the **set to** block between the **when flag clicked** and **forever if touching ball** blocks.

9. Change the value from **Score** to **Steps**.

10. Click the flag and play the game. The score and the paddle steps variables increment as you play.

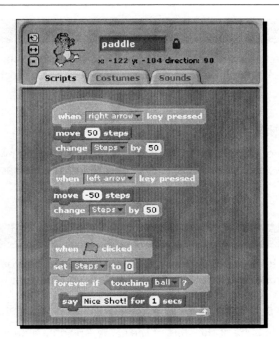

What just happened?

Each time I pressed an arrow key, my sprite moved 50 steps and the paddle steps monitor on the stage incremented by 50. If your sprite moved a different number of steps, you can change the value of the Steps variable accordingly.

When we added the Steps variable to the paddle, we noticed that we couldn't access the variable from any other sprite. When we clicked on the **ball** sprite, for example, the Steps variable was not an option. Also, when the Steps monitor displayed on the stage, it displayed as **paddle Steps**, which was another indicator that we were working with a local variable.

Global versus local variables

All sprites can change the value of a global variable; therefore, it can be difficult to track problems when they occur because we have to investigate each script in each sprite to find all the places that may be affecting our project. The bigger our project gets, the harder it can be to keep track of global variables.

We may also program in some unintended consequences, such as adding 50 points to our score each time we press the right arrow key, when what we really want to do is only count the number of steps.

Have a go hero

In the next exercise, we will introduce a second ball into the game. Your task is to add a new sprite to the project and name it **ball2**. In addition, you need to duplicate the ball's scripts for the **ball2** sprite.

Add a second level

Let's add another level of complexity to our pong game by adding a new level that triggers based on elapsed time. After 30 seconds, we're going to introduce a second ball to the game.

Let's begin now.

Time for action – reach for a new level

If you did the previous hero exercise, then you have a second ball in your project. If you didn't do the hero exercise, you'll need to finish it before you can continue:

1. Select **ball2** from the sprites list so we can begin customizing it.

2. We need to hide **ball2** at the start of the game, so add a **hide** block between the **when flag clicked** and the **go to** blocks.

3. Next, we want to display **ball2** after 30 seconds has elapsed. From the **Control** palette, add a **wait until** block between the **go to** and **wait until touching color red** blocks.

4. From the **Operators** palette, add the **greater than** block (see the following screenshot) to the input value of the **wait until** block we just added to the script.

5. Our **greater than** block needs two values. For the first value, add the **timer** block from the **Sensing** palette. Then, select the checkbox next to the **timer** block to report the time on the stage.

6. For the second value in our **greater than** block, type **30**.

7. After the timer is greater than 30 block, we need to show **ball2**. Add a **show** block between the two **wait until** blocks.

8. Set the direction of the ball. From the **Motion** palette, add the **point in direction** block between the **show** and the **go to** blocks. Change the value to **-45**.

9. We need to ensure that the timer starts from 0 at the start of each game. Select the **Stage**. From the **Sensing** palette, add the **reset timer** block between the **when flag clicked** and **forever** blocks.

10. Click the flag and play the game. After 30 seconds, the second ball will display.

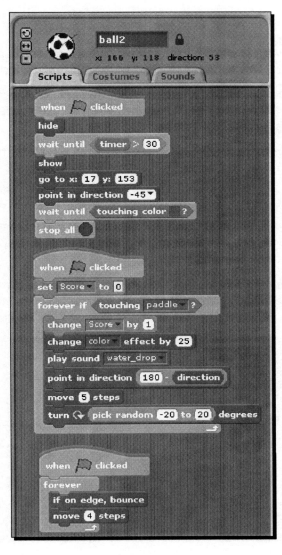

What just happened?

If we were good enough, we lasted for 30 seconds and advanced to the next level in our game.

To determine when we reached level two, we did a simple arithmetic problem. We waited until the value of the timer was greater than 30 until we showed ball2. After ball2 displayed on the stage, the **point in direction** block set the ball's initial path to **-45**.

We reset the timer to **0** because the timer continually runs without any regard to the rest of the project. If we didn't reset it to **0**, then our game would always start with two balls. That's not the objective.

Comparisons

Scratch includes three ways in which we can compare values: greater than, less than, or equal to. We can compare any combination of constant and variable values, including two variables.

When Scratch compares two values, it returns either true or false. The statement 5 = 4 returns false, while 6 < 10 returns true. Remember, when we use a variable for one of the values, the variable really contains a number.

If we compare values within a conditional statement, Scratch executes the code only if the statement is true.

Troubleshooting

If you played long enough, you might have discovered a bug in our program. Sometimes when the balls collide, the program stops running, and sometimes the balls appear to pass through each other without any problems.

Can you determine the problem? My first thought was that the X and Y coordinates of the two balls matched. The following screenshot shows a scenario where my scripts stopped running, unexpectedly. However, the coordinates of the two balls are clearly different.

What do we know about the reason our scripts stop running? We have a code associated with ball2 that says, **wait until ball2 touches the color red**, then stop all scripts. If you look at the previous screenshot, what color shows on the ball? The color red is displayed.

Time for action – fix the script

We can fix our problem in any number of ways. We could replace the red stripe with a new sprite and make the game end when one of the balls touches the sprite. In the following exercise, we're going to test two conditions to determine if the game should end:

1. Select the **ball2** sprite from the list of sprites.

2. Drag the **touching color red** block out of the **wait until** block and place it somewhere in the scripts area. We'll use it again in a moment.

3. From the **Operators** palette, drag the **and** block into the **wait until** block.

4. Drag the **touching color red** block into the first value of the **and** block.

5. Now, we need a way to exclude the times when **ball2** touches the red ball. From the **Operators** palette, drag the **not** block into the second value of the **and** block.

6. Let's add the exclusion. From the **Sensing** palette, drag the **touching** block into the value of the **not** block.

7. Select **ball** from the drop-down list. Our revised code looks like the following screenshot:

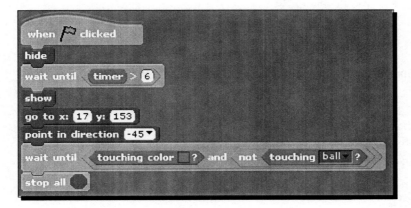

8. Play the game to test the solution.

9. If you're satisfied with this fix, duplicate it on the other **ball** sprite.

What just happened?

We previously had two conditions that gave us a red color, and that caused problems. As the balls flew around the stage, ball2 continually evaluated if it touched the color red. Now, if ball2 touched red, it also evaluated whether or not it is touching the other ball.

In human speak, we would say if the ball touched the color red and the other ball, do nothing; however, if the ball touched the color red while not touching the other ball, stop all scripts.

Using Boolean logic

When we use conditional statements, we can incorporate Boolean logic to determine whether or not we should run the code. The Boolean operators are the **and** block, the **or** block, and the **not** bock. They can all be found in the **Operators** palette.

If you want to ensure that two conditions are met, use the **and** block. If only one of two conditions need to be met at any given time, use the **or** block.

The **not** block checks whether a specified condition is met or not. And if the condition is not met, it returns a value of true. A true value triggers the conditional statement to run.

Pop quiz

1. If you want to create a variable for a sprite's exclusive use, which of the following options do you select when creating the variable?
    - For all sprites
    - Not for this sprite
    - For all sprites but this one
    - For this sprite only

2. Which of the following blocks is not a Boolean operator?
    - wait
    - or
    - and
    - not

Add levels

We programmed the logic to create levels. Now, let's add a visual indicator to count the levels.

Time for action – count the levels

We'll add our levels to the stage:

1. With the stage selected, create a new variable called **Level**.

2. From the **Variables** palette, add the **set to** block between the **reset timer** and the **forever** blocks. Select **Level** from the drop-down list.

3. Change the value of the **set level** block to **1**.

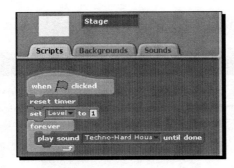

4. Now, we need to increment the level when the second ball enters the stage. Select **ball2** from the sprites list.

5. Add the **change Level by 1** block between the **wait until timer > 30** and the **show** blocks.

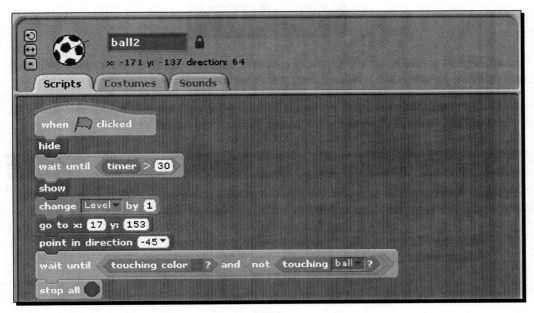

6. Right-click on the **timer** block on the stage and select **hide**. We don't need to see the timer anymore.

7. Play the game and after 30 seconds, the Level increases by one.

What just happened?

We built the visual representation of the levels based on the programming we previously created. The level changed when we introduced the second ball, which happened after 30 seconds of game play.

Level two is currently infinite.

Have a go hero

What ideas do you have for creating levels? How about if you increase the ball speed for each additional level? For each ball, you need to adjust the number of steps the sprite moves when it bounces off the edge of the stage. See the following screenshot for a hint:

This will require you to rework the current scripts so that you can calculate a new number of steps to move based on the level and then store that new value in a variable.

You will also need a way to increment levels beyond what we have created. Time may not be the best option. Perhaps changing levels based on the score would be better.

Time for action – enter project notes

The project notes provides us a place to give our players some more information about the game, and in our case, we need to provide attribution for our project:

1. From the **File** menu, select the **Show project notes** option to display the **Project Notes** dialog box.

2. Type your notes about the game, such as instructions, known issues, and in our case we want to state that we modified an existing Scratch project.

3. When you've finished entering notes, click **OK**.

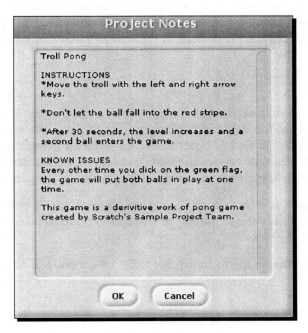

What just happened?

It took only a minute to provide some minimal documentation about our project, but our users will thank us for the information later.

 The project notes also display in the Open Project dialog box.

Most importantly, we provided credit for our work. Even though our finished game doesn't look much like the game we started out with, much of the original code is in use.

Next steps

This game has a bug that makes both balls display at one time, but it happens only every other time the flag is clicked. And it happens only if both balls displayed in the previous game. Can you fix it?

There are a lot of possibilities with our pong game. We could build more levels with additional sprites or with sprites that appear and reappear. By now, you probably have a handful of ways to improve this game. Feel free to change it up.

Of course, the concepts we've used in this chapter can be combined with everything we've learned so far to create an entirely different game of your own design. If you need some additional game ideas, browse the projects in the **Games** folder that is included with Scratch.

Summary

The centerpiece of our pong project was dynamic data, and we've identified several ways we can interact with and use those dynamic values to create a game. We examined several of Scratch's built-in variables as well as created our own variables to track score and level. The variables became the input for various conditional checks that determined whether or not something else happened, such as a second ball being added to the game.

We also demonstrated some techniques to help troubleshoot problems. In addition to analyzing our code, we used the single stepping option in Scratch to understand what our code was doing, block by block.

In the next chapter, we'll visit the fortune teller while we continue to explore variable data in list format.

7

Games of Fortune

In Chapter 6, we learned how easy it is to create projects that incorporate dynamic information using variables. However, variables have a limitation; they store only one value at a time. Sometimes, we want a variable to store multiple values.

Welcome to lists. In Scratch, a list allows us to associate one list (a variable) with multiple items or values in much the same way we create a list before going to the grocery store.

In this chapter, we will take a trip to the fortune-teller to demonstrate lists, and I predict you'll learn how to:

- ◆ Store and retrieve information in lists
- ◆ Keep track of items in a list by using a counter
- ◆ Identify intervals using the **mod** block
- ◆ Use if/else control blocks to make decisions
- ◆ Ask the user a question and store the keyboard input

That's a lot to process, but we can do it.

Fortune-teller

Most of us enjoy a good circus, carnival, or county fair. There's fun, food, and fortunes. Aah, yes, what would a fair be without the fortune-teller's tent? By the end of the chapter, you'll know everything you need to spin your fortunes and amaze your friends with your wisdom.

Before we start the first exercise, create a new project and add two sprites. The first sprite will be the seeker. The second sprite will be the teller. Choose any sprites you want. My seeker will be a clam and my teller will be a snowman. If you want to add a background, go ahead.

Time for action – create a list of questions

In order to have a successful fortune-telling, we need two things: a question and an answer. Let's start by defining some questions and answers:

1. Select the **seeker** from the list of sprites.

2. From the **Variables** palette, click the **Make a list** button.

3. In the list name dialog box, type **questions** and select **For this sprite only**.

4. Click **OK** to create the list. Several new blocks display in the **Variables** palette, and an empty block titled **seeker questions** displays on the stage.

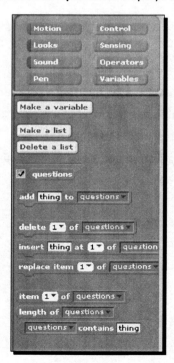

5. Let's think about a couple of questions we may be tempted to ask, such as the following:

   ◆ Will my hair fall out?

   ◆ How many children will I have?

6. Let's add our proposed questions to the questions list. Click the **plus sign** located in the bottom-left corner of the seeker questions box (on the stage) to display a text input field. Type **Will my hair fall out?**

7. Press the plus sign again and enter the second question: **How many children will I have?** We now have two questions in our list.

[To automatically add the next item in the list, press enter.]

8. Let's add a **say for 2 secs** block to the scripts area of the **seeker** sprite so that we can start the dialog.

9. From the **Variables** palette, drag the **item of questions** block to the input value of the **say for 2 secs** block.

10. Double-click on the block and the seeker asks, "**Will my hair fall out?**"

11. Change the value on the **item** block to **last** and double-click the block again. This time the seeker asks, "**How many children will I have?**"

What just happened?

I'm certain you could come up with a hundred different questions to ask a fortune-teller. Don't worry, you'll get your chance to ask more questions later.

Did you notice that the new list we created behaved a lot like a variable? We were able to make the questions list private; we don't want our teller to peek at our questions, after all. Also, the list became visible on the screen allowing us to edit the contents.

The most notable difference is that we added more than one item, and each item corresponds to a number. We essentially created a numbered list.

 If you work with other programming languages, then you might refer to lists as arrays.

Because the seeker's questions were contained in a list, we used the **item** block to provide special instructions to the **say** block in order to ask the question. The first value of the **item** block was position, which defaulted to one. The second value was the name of the list, which defaulted to questions.

In contrast, if we used a variable to store a question, we would only need to supply the name of the variable to the **say** block. We saw those examples in Chapter 6.

Have a go hero

Create an answers list for the **teller** sprite, and add several items to the list. Remember, there are no wrong answers in this exercise.

Work with an item in a list

We can use lists to group related items, but accessing the items in the list requires an extra level of specificity. We need to know the name of the list and the position of the item within the list before we can do anything with the values.

The following table shows the available ways to access a specific item in a list.

Position	Description	Uses
First	Identifies the first item in the list.	Insert, delete, replace, or retrieve the first item in the list.
Any	Selects a random item in the list.	Insert, replace, or retrieve a random item in the list.
Last	Selects the last item in the list.	Insert, delete, replace, or retrieve the last item in the list.

Position	Description	Uses
Variable	Specifies a variable that contains a number instead of the default first, any, or last values.	Use the variable to store the position of an item in the list, then insert, delete, replace, retrieve the item that corresponds to the value.
Manual input	Enters a specific item number.	Insert, delete, replace, or retrieve a constant item number, such as item 5.

Import a list

Entering one item at a time via the Scratch interface is functional, but the small size of the list box can be difficult to use when we need to add a large number of items. Fortunately, we can create a text file outside of Scratch and then import it into our list.

Before you continue with the exercise, build your own text file with the fortunes you want to use in response to the seeker's questions. Enter one fortune per line in a text editor, such as Notepad.

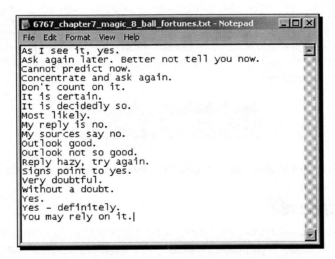

You can use any fortunes you want, but I'm going to use a list of common Magic 8 ball responses that I found on Wikipedia at http://en.wikipedia.org/wiki/Magic_8_ball. My list will contain 19 items to start.

Time for action – import a list of fortunes

If you haven't already done so, create a new list and name it **answers**.

1. To import the list, right-click on the answers list and choose **import...** Note: This will erase any items you previously added to the answers list.

2. In the **Import List** dialog box, browse to the fortunes file you saved on your computer prior to starting this exercise and import it.

3. Think of a new fortune that is not yet in your answers list. We are going to add it to the list. I'll use "No comment" as my new fortune.

4. Now, let's add the new fortune to our list. From the Variables palette, find the **add** block. Replace the default value **thing** with your new fortune. Make sure the answers list is selected.

5. Double-click on the **add** block to add the new item to the end of the answers list.

What just happened?

I don't know about you, but I had a much easier time typing in a text editor than I did typing in the list monitor. Actually, if you took my lead, you copied the Magic 8 ball® responses from Wikipedia and pasted them into a text file. That way, all you had to do was to clean up some formatting.

We did add a new fortune to the list via the **add** block. The **add** block always places the new value at the end of the list. Now, my list contains 20 items. As an alternative, we could have updated the original fortunes text file and then re-imported the list.

Reasons to import

It's true that importing a list makes list creation easy. However, we can use the Import List functionality in other creative ways. For example, we could create a game that instructs the player to create a unique list that he or she can import into Scratch. That way, each player can customize the game.

If we create a math game, we could ask the player for a varied set of numbers to make the problems different. You get the idea.

Export a list

Sometimes, we may want to export a list from Scratch to a file. For example, as people play a game, we may want to collect all the scores into a separate list that we can later export to a text file on our computer.

As we create our projects, the contents of a list may change from the original list we imported. In that case, we may want to export the new list.

To export a list, right-click on the list monitor and click **export**. The file automatically saves to the root installation directory for Scratch. In Windows, that is `C:\Program Files\Scratch`.

Pop quiz

1. If you wanted to group ten related items together, you would create a new:
   - Variable
   - Numbers block
   - List
   - Forever loop

2. If you want to add many items to a list at one time, how would you do it?
   - Type each item one at a time into the **add** block
   - Type each item into the list monitor that displays on the stage
   - Export the list from Scratch
   - Create a list in a text file and import it via Scratch

Your fortune is ...

Take a moment to add more questions to the **seeker** sprite's question list.

Now that we have a list of several questions for our seeker to ask and a list of fortunes for our teller to answer, let's create the script that randomly selects a question.

Time for action – tell me a fortune

Before we begin, hide the lists from the stage by right-clicking on each list and selecting **hide** so that they are out of the way. Let's start with the **seeker** sprite. We should have a **say** block in the scripts area from our earlier exercise:

1. We need a way to control our seeker. From the **Control** palette, drag the **when space key pressed** block and attach it to the **say** block.

2. From the position drop-down list in the **item** block, select **any**. Press the space key to ask a question. Each time you press the space key, a random question from the list displays.

3. We need to let the teller know we've asked a question, and that we expect an answer. From the **Control** palette, add the **broadcast** block.

4. Add a new broadcast message titled **fortune**.

5. Every question deserves an answer. Select the **teller** sprite so that we can create the script to provide an answer.

6. From the **Control** palette, drag the **when I receive** block into the scripts area, and make sure **fortune** displays as the message value.

7. From the **Looks** palette, add the **say for 2 secs** block to the **when I receive** block.

8. Let's pick a random item from the answers list. From the **Variables** palette, add the **item** block as the input to the **say** block.

9. For the **seeker** sprite, we pick a random question using the **any** position of the **item** block. This time, we're going to take a slightly different approach to build a more flexible, but slightly more complicated script. From the **Operators** palette, add the **pick random** block as the position value of the **item** block.

10. From the **Variables** palette, add the **length of** block to the second value of the **pick random** block. Make sure the answers list is selected for the value in the **length of** block. The following screenshot shows the script for the **teller** sprite:

11. Press the Space bar to make the seeker ask a question. The teller will respond with a fortune.

 Every item in a list is represented by a number, and when we want to manipulate a certain value in the list, it's the number we refer to. The **list length** block gives us a way to always know how many items are in a list. In our example, our list of answers contains 20 items.

What just happened?

You are now prepared for a life in the carnival. Based on our script, we can answer any question that may come our way, and our response will seem profound. At least that's what we'll choose to believe.

Our seeker asked a question, and our teller doled out a random fortune using items from their respective lists. The script we used for the **teller** sprite was decidedly more complex than the script for the **seeker** sprite.

In the seeker's script, we used the default **any** value to select a random item from the list. For the teller, we replaced the **any** value with a **pick random** block. The **length of questions** block gave the **pick random** block the maximum number of items to choose from. In my example, the script selected a number between 1 and 20 because my questions list contained 20 items.

You're probably asking yourself why we would write the more complex code when we can achieve the same result with less. If you are asking that question, good for you.

The answer, naturally, depends on what we want to accomplish. If we only want to select a random item from our list, then the simple script for the seeker suffices. However, let's say we want to instruct our teller to answer every fifth question with a positive response, and all other questions get a random response.

Let's see how we can modify the teller's script to guarantee a positive fortune for every fifth question.

Time for action – force a positive fortune

Before we begin this exercise, re-order your answers list so that all the positive responses are at the end. Edit the list items in your text editor and then re-import the list. Make a note of where the first positive response begins:

1. Our first task is to set up a variable to count how many questions the seeker asks so that we can calculate whether or not it's time to answer positively. Select the **stage** from the sprites list and create a new variable named **question_number.**

 We add the variable to stage because both sprites will use the variable, and when we create a variable on the stage it's always a global variable.

2. Add the **when flag clicked** block to the scripts area.

3. From the **Variables** palette, add the **set question_number to 0** block to the **when flag clicked** block. Now, we have a way to reset our calculation.

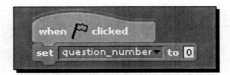

4. Next, we need to assign the **question_number** variable a value when the seeker asks a question. Click on the **seeker** sprite to display the scripts area.

5. From the **Variables** palette, snap the **change question_number by 1** block in place between the **when space key pressed** and the **say** blocks.

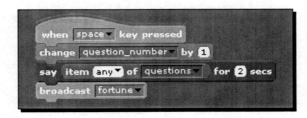

6. Next, make the **teller** sprite give a specific range of answers based on the question. Select the **teller** sprite to display the scripts area.

7. From the **Control** palette, add the **if/else** block to the **when I receive** block. Snap the current **say** block in place after the **if** block.

8. Change the first input value on the **pick random** block to reflect the item number that begins your positive responses. In my example, that value is 11.

9. Now, we need to supply a condition to the **if** statement to test whether or not we should issue a positive response. From the **Operators** palette, add the **=** block to the **if** block.

10. Drag the **mod** block into the value to the left of the **=** sign. Change the value to the right of the equals sign to **0**.

11. We're going to use the **mod** block to divide **question_number** by 5 so that we can calculate the remainder. Add the **question_number** block to the first value of the **mod** block.

12. Change the second value of the **mod** block to **5** so that the block reads **question_number mod 5**.

13. Test your script by pressing the Space bar. With our current setup, the teller responds only on the fifth question, and it's always a positive response.

If you double-click on the variable monitor block on the stage, a slider will display. Use the slider to assign a number to the variable before you run the script as a way to test.

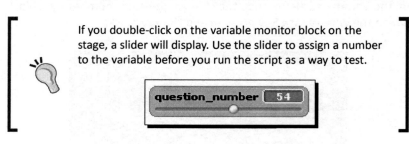

What just happened?

We asked our teller to issue only a positive response every fifth question, but we needed a way to let our **teller** sprite determine when the fifth question was asked. We set up the **question_number** variable as a way to count the question, and the seeker script updated the value of the **question_number** variable each time we pressed the space key. We call that a counter variable.

The **mod** block gave us the logic we needed to let the teller calculate whether or not to issue a positive response. The **mod** block divided the first number (**question_number**) by the second (**5**) and returned the remainder.

The **teller** sprite used the **if** block to compare the remainder to zero. We chose zero because when question_number is a multiple of 5, the remainder was zero. When the remainder was zero, we executed the code in the **if** block; otherwise, the code in the **else** block ran.

Let's evaluate some mod calculations using a divisor of 5:

◆ 25 mod 5 is 0
◆ 32 mod 5 is 2
◆ 67 mod 5 is 3

In our script, question 25 guarantees a positive response, while questions 32 and 67 do not.

Counters

When we need to know how many items we've processed like we did in our "force a positive fortune" exercise, we use a counter variable. A counter variable is just an arbitrary name I chose so that we can easily associate that we are using a variable to count the steps in some process.

For example, iterating through each item in a list is a common example of using a variable to count the current list item's position. Consider the block of code in the following screenshot:

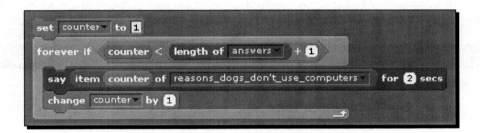

Imagine if we had used a list to store our jokes in Chapter 5. Our scripts would have been much simpler to construct. The sample code in the screenshot uses the counter variable in several ways. It sets the value to 1 prior to checking the condition in the **forever if** block. It uses the number assigned to counter to determine if we've processed all the items in the list. If counter is less than the number of items in the list, the block runs. At the end of the block, we increment counter's value by 1, and the **forever if** block checks the new value of counter.

Keep track of intervals with mod

If we identify an interval, then we can create a pattern of events based on the interval. We already saw an example where we look for the fifth occurrence of an event, but what if we wanted to make our sprite dance after 100 seconds elapse? A mod calculation helps us identify the interval. Assuming our timer starts at zero, the expression "current_time mod 100 is 0" becomes a check to identify every 100th second.

In our project example, we used the **mod** block to select certain items from our list, but we could program any number of events based on our interval, such as select items from a totally different list, change backgrounds or costumes, or we could use the mod calculation to do nothing at all.

Have a go hero

Give mod a try. Make the **seeker** sprite do something on every fifth response. Examples of things you might try include issuing a response to the teller, applying a graphical transformation, or jumping for joy.

If/else

In earlier chapters, we became familiar with **forever**, **forever if**, and **if** concepts. Each of these concepts checks a condition and then runs if the condition is met. We don't define what happens when the condition is not met.

In contrast, the **if/else** control block evaluates a condition, and if the evaluation is true, the code in the **if** block executes. If the **if** condition evaluates to false, then the code in the **else** block executes.

Think of the ultimatums you give your children, or your parents gave you. If you clean your room, you get ice cream. Or else, you go to bed without a snack.

Pop quiz

1. The **mod** block:
   - Modifies a number in the list
   - Creates a variable that tracks an interval
   - Transforms the sprite into a leprechaun
   - Divides two numbers and returns the remainder

2. We use a counter variable to:
   - Track how many times an event occurs
   - Identify how many sprites we have in the project
   - Select a random item from a list
   - Add a new item to a specific position in the list

Repeat the fortune

Up to this point, we've only stored numeric values in our variables, but variables can store text too. Let's add a script to our **teller** sprite to repeat the question.

Time for action – my fortune is what?

What if we get distracted and miss our fortune? That would be tragic, so let's add some code to the **teller** sprite that repeats the last fortune told:

1. Create a private variable for the **teller** sprite named **your_fortune**. We'll use this variable to keep track of the fortune.

2. We'll start with the blocks inside the **if** statement. From the **Variables** palette, snap the **set to** block in place between the **if** block and the **say** block. Select **your_fortune** as the variable so that the block reads **set your_fortune to 0**.

3. We need to replace the **0** value in the **set to** block with the code that selects a random item from the answers list. Remember, we're working with the **if** block right now. Click on the **item** block and drag the entire block into the **to** value of the **set to** block.

4. From the **Variables** palette, drag the **your_fortune** block into the value of the **say** block. Refer to the following screenshot for the new script:

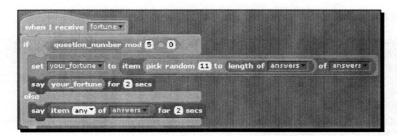

5. Apply the same changes to the **else** block. Refer to the following screenshot for help:

6. Get a fortune by pressing the Space bar. Notice that the your_fortune monitor reports the teller's fortune.

7. Now, we need a way to prompt the teller to repeat the message. We'll add a **when clicked** control block to the **teller** sprite. From the **Control** palette, add the **when teller clicked** block to the scripts area.

8. From the Looks palette, add the **say for 2 secs** block to the **when teller clicked** block.

9. From the Variables palette, add the **your_fortune** block as the message value for the **say** block.

10. Click the **teller** sprite to repeat the last fortune.

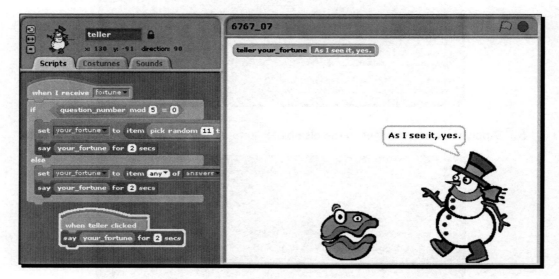

What just happened?

Like thoughts, fortunes can be fleeting. That's why we captured our fortune in the **your_fortune** variable. We replaced where in our script we selected the fortune. Our logic to pick a random item from the answers list became the input to the **set to** block. And for the **say** block, we replaced the message value with the **your_fortune** variable.

Now, if we get a fortune we like, we can make the teller repeat it over and over.

Holding text in a variable

In earlier chapters, we typed text directly into the **say** block. This means that if we want to change what the sprite says, we have to find the **say** block in the script and change the message.

When we work with dynamic data, we sometimes want to capture that data so that we can use it later. We already learned how we can use variables to store numeric data, but having the ability to store text adds a whole new level of functionality to our projects, such as simulating dynamic conversations.

 Other programming languages often refer to a text phrase as a **string**.

Variables are one of the most important programming concepts we can use. A majority of the projects you create will need a variable, especially as the projects become more interactive and complex.

Do you have a question?

Now is a logical time to build some audience participation into our game, so we're going to prompt the user for a question via the **ask** block. After the user types the question, the teller sprite will provide the fortune.

The ability to collect a string of text via the keyboard is new in Scratch 1.4.

Time for action – ask your question

Select the seeker sprite, and let's begin.

1. From the Control palette, add the **when seeker clicked** block to the scripts area.

2. From the Sensing palette, add the **ask** block to the **when seeker clicked** block.

3. Type a question in the **ask** block. This is the question, the sprite seeker will ask.

4. Add a **broadcast** block to the script and select the message **fortune**.

5. Click the **seeker** to display the ask box on the stage.

6. Type your question, and then either click the check mark on the ask field or press Enter on your keyboard. The teller responds with your fortune.

What just happened?

Let's hope our teller believes in the old mantra, "there are no dumb questions."

When we clicked on the teller, the seeker used a speech bubble to ask the question we defined in the **ask** block. In my example, the seeker's question was "Ask your question."

The **ask** block forces the script to wait for keyboard input, which means our project stopped until we provided input into the ask box. When we pressed the Enter key, the **broadcast** block woke the teller up, and we got our fortune.

Add the question to the list

The keyboard input gets stored in the **answers** variable, which can be found in the Sensing palette. We're going to use the **answers** variable along with additional string operators to add each new question to the seekers **questions** list.

Time for action – add it to the list

Because we want to avoid duplicates, we're going to check to see if the value in the **answer** block exists in the **questions** list.

1. Add the **if** block to the when seeker clicked script.

2. From the Operators palette, add the **not** block as the condition to check in the **if** block.

3. From the Variables palette, add the **contains** block to the **not** block. Select the **questions** list from the drop down.

4. Next, add the **answers** block from the Sensing palette to the **contains** block.

 The **answer** block is a reporter, which means you can display its value on the stage by selecting it from the Sensing palette. You can also see its value by single clicking on the **answer** block.

5. If the **questions** list doesn't contain the answer, add it to the list. From the Variables palette, add the **add to** block to the **if** block. Select **questions** from the drop down.

6. Add the **answers** block to the **add to** block. Your script should look like the following screen shot.

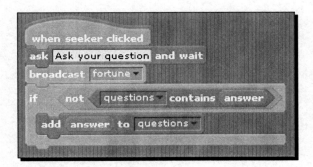

Test your script by typing answers that exist in the questions list and by typing answers that don't exist in the list. You can monitor the values in the questions list by turning on the **questions** reporter block in the Variables palette.

What just happened?

The **not** operator made our conditional statement read, "If the answer is not contained in the list, then add it to the questions list." By comparing the value in the **answer** block to any value in the **questions** block, we were able to determine whether or not we should add the answer to the list.

Join two text phrases

Not only did Scratch 1.4 give us the ability to capture keyboard input for use in our scripts, it allows us to perform additional operations, such as joining two text phrases together.

Time for action – join two sentences

For every question the seeker asks, the teller has a response. Let's use the join block to add a little "thoughtfulness" to the response.

1. The current teller script uses a **say** block to repeat the fortune in the **if/else** block. Replace the second instance of the **your_fortune** block with the **join** block from the Operators palette. See the following screen shot.

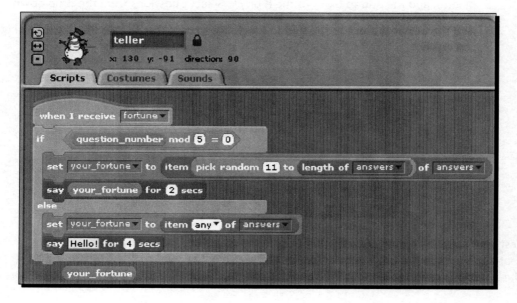

2. Type a greeting into the first field of the join block. My example uses "That's an interesting question."

3. Add the **your_fortune** block to the second field of the **join** block.

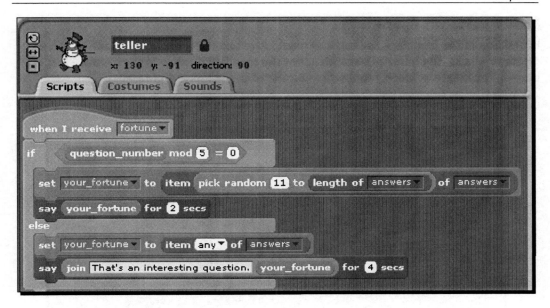

Run the script several times to test the code to observe the teller's response. Remember, we previously built this script to provide a different answer on every fifth question, which means our new code will not always run.

What just happened?

Using the **join** block, we combined a constant phrase with the phrase contained in the **your_fortune** block, a variable. We could have achieved the same results with **say** blocks, but we would have needed to use two **say** blocks to accomplish the same thing. Also, the **join** block gave the script a different tempo than what we would have been able to achieve using multiple **say** blocks.

Nest join blocks

Like many other blocks in Scratch, we can nest multiple join blocks. This allows us to join multiple text phrases to form complex thoughts and paragraphs, as the following screenshot demonstrates.

Additional string operations

In addition to the **join** block, we can also manipulate text using the **letter of** and **length of** Operator blocks. The **letter of** block identifies the specified position in the supplied text phrase. The **length of** block, reports the number of characters in a phrase.

Consider the following screen shot, which is a help screen from Scratch.

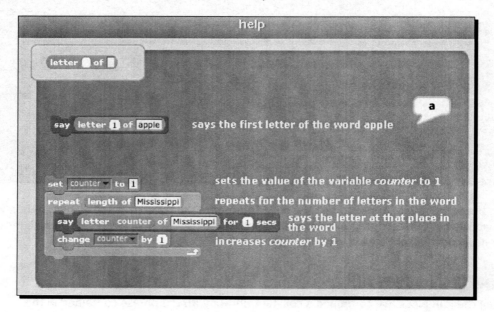

We can also use the comparison blocks, (>, <, and =) to evaluate one string against another. Consider the following screen shot.

The code in the screen shot checks to see if the keyboard input in the **answer** block, matches any of the items in the **questions** list. Just like comparing two numbers, if a match is made, the statement evaluates to true; otherwise it's false.

Next steps

Our focus has been on using lists and variables to drive the action in our game. If you wanted to expand on this game, try adding graphical effects to the sprites and creating a design that begins to tell a story.

Using the concepts in this chapter, you could create other games of chance, such as blackjack, bingo, or a lottery number predictor. The text operators give you a lot of flexibility to create more complex and natural conversations.

Summary

We have seen the power that lists and variables give us to create dynamic, flexible, and fun projects. As you worked through this chapter, you probably realized that we could have used lists in some of our previous projects. For example, our scripts in Chapter 5 would have been much smaller had we used lists.

We learned how to manipulate lists, a special kind of variable, to collect a group of related items. We continued to explore variables by using them to store text. The **mod** block helped us identify intervals as we iterated through our list. We used a variable to keep track of the interval so that we could program specific events based on when an interval occurred.

When we're working with text, it's natural to want to capture keyboard input from our user and then use that text in our scripts. Thanks to the new features in Scratch 1.4, we saw how easy it was to incorporate test strings from the user.

Our programming knowledge has been accumulating nicely to this point even though you may not know it. We're ready to apply everything we've learned, plus more, in our next project. Get your money.

8

Math and Finance

If I offered you $15,000 or one dollar that doubled every day for 30 days, which one would you choose? By the time we finish the chapter, you'll know if you've chosen wisely.

We'll use the Indian folktale by Demi, "One Grain of Rice," to inspire our project and to demonstrate the power of doubling. In the folktale, a village girl asks a greedy king to double a single grain of rice each day for thirty days as a way to accumulate enough rice to feed the hungry villagers.

In this chapter, we will illustrate the math behind the folktale and compare it to conventional interest-based accrual methods. Specifically, we will:

- ◆ *Calculate the total amount of money if we double a dollar each day*
- ◆ *Collect user input via slider input controls*
- ◆ *Graph the results of a calculation using the pen and stamp tools*
- ◆ *Build interactive math problems using variables*
- ◆ *Calculate simple interest on an amount of money*

I'm using dollars as the basis for my project, but the math works whether we use euros, rice, or chicken legs.

Double it or lump sum?

Let's refine our problem statement to include an interest calculation: Would you rather earn 4% interest on $15,000 for one month or receive $1 that doubles every day for 15 days?

To help us make the right choice, we will do both calculations. We'll show the results of the doubled amount using a graph, and we'll use a sprite to report the interest amount.

We'll build some user-input features into each calculation so that the user can experiment with variable amounts.

We'll begin by setting up the equation to calculate the doubled amount and its graph.

Double it

The doubling formula is relatively simple. Day two's value is twice as much as day one's. Day three's is twice as much as day two's, and on and on it goes.

We can represent the math with this equation:

newAmount = startAmount x 2

Before you begin, create a new sprite in the shape of a circle. The ellipsis tool in the Paint Editor works well for this. We'll use this sprite to draw the points on our graph, so make it relatively small. Name the sprite **double**.

Time for action – calculate the double amount

We'll continue to use our knowledge of variables to build an equation where we can change each value, each time:

1. Define the variables. For the **double** sprite, create the following for this sprite only variables: newAmount, startAmount, days, and count.

2. Let's build the equation. From the **Variables** palette, add the **set to** block to the **double** sprite's scripts area. Change the variable in the **set to** block to **newAmount**.

3. We want to set the **newAmount** value equal to the **startAmount**. Drag the **startAmount** variable into the second value of the **set to** block.

4. Right now, our calculation represents day one. We'll use a **forever if** block to calculate the remaining days. From the **Control** palette, wrap a **forever if** block around the **set to** block.

5. The number of times we double the value will depend on the value assigned to the **days** variable. We'll use the **count** variable as a way to control whether or not we need to calculate one more day or stop the calculation. From the **Operators** palette, drag the **<** block into the conditional value of the **forever if** block.

6. From the **Variables** palette, drag the **count** block into the first conditional value of the **<** block. Drag the **days** block into the second value of the **<** block.

7. We need to reset our counter. Add a **set to** block between the existing **set newAmount to startAmount** and **forever if** blocks. Select **count** from the drop-down list and type **1** as the new value.

8. Now, let's do the math inside the loop. Add a **set to** block inside the **forever if** block. Select **newAmount** from the drop-down list.

9. To calculate the new amount, we need to take the previous new amount and multiply it by 2. From the **Operators** palette, add the * block to the **set newAmount to** block.

10. Drag the **newAmount** block into the first value in the * block, and type **2** in the second value of the * block.

11. After we run through the **forever if** block one time, we need to increment the **count** variable by 1. Add the **change by** block to the end of the **forever if** block. Select **count** from the list of variables, and type the number **1** for the "by" value.

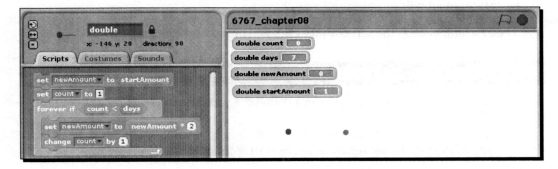

Check your script against the screenshot to make sure your blocks match.

Before we run our code, let's take a look at what our code is supposed to do. Then, we'll test it and see if we've succeeded.

What just happened?

Almost every value in our script is represented by a variable that we can change. Unfortunately, all our variables default to 0, so eventually we will need to define our variables. First, let's examine our calculation.

We assumed that we always want to calculate the value for at least one day. Our first calculation outside the if block sets the **newAmount** variable equal to the **startAmount**, and then it incremented the **count** variable by one. This is the only place we used the **startAmount** variable in our script.

Starting with day two, the calculation inside the **forever if** block, we took a shortcut in our math by multiplying **newAmount** by two..

After each calculation, we increment the **count** variable by one so that the conditional statement in the forever if block can determine if more calculations are necessary. The **forever if** block compares **count** to **days** and, if **count** is less than **days**, it calculates a new value.

As we work through the chapter, we will allow the user to set both the **startAmount** and the **days** variables prior to running the calculation.

Have a go hero

Set the default values for the **count**, **days**, **newAmount**, and **startAmount** variables by using the **when flag clicked** control block. Use the following values:

◆ count = 0
◆ days = 7
◆ startAmount = 1
◆ newAmount = 0

If you need a hint, peek at the screenshot at the end of the next exercise.

Time for action – set user-defined variables

We need to know if our script works, so let's define the variables to values other than zero:

1. Add a control block to our calculation script. Snap the **when space bar pressed** block onto the top of the **set newAmount to startAmount** block.

2. Now, test the work you did in the hero exercise. Click the **flag** to reset the values of each variable so that count equals 0, days equals 7, startAmount equals 1, and newAmount equals 0.

3. Press the Space bar to calculate the amount of money you would have if you started with one dollar and doubled it every day for seven days. The value in **newAmount** is **64**.

4. Let's give the user the ability to set a starting amount. Find the **startAmount** monitor on the screen and double-click it to display a slider. You may need to drag the monitor block around the screen if it's covered up by another monitor.

5. We want to make our numbers are manageable, so let's limit the range of numbers we accept. Right-click on the **startAmount** monitor and choose **set slider min and max**.

6. In the **Slider range** dialog box, enter **1** for the min value and **5** for the **Max** value. Click **OK**.

7. Now, drag the slider slowly to the right and note that, as you move, the value increases, but it does not exceed a maximum value of 5 or a minimum value of 1.

8. Run the script several times using several values for newAmount, and test the results.

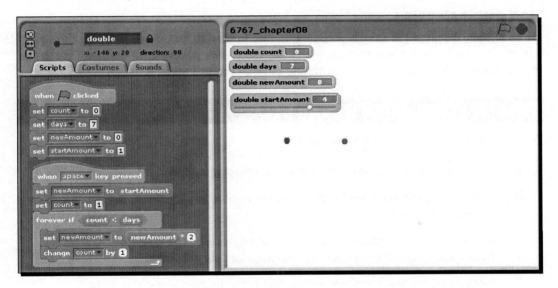

As you run the script, don't forget to click the flag to reset your calculations. Enter a new startAmount and press the Space bar to calculate the value.

What just happened?

If you look at the monitor blocks on the stage, you'll notice every block has a value. Did you notice a pattern in your calculation? If not, rerun the script using the values 1, 2, and 4. If we double the **startAmount**, the **newAmount** doubles as well.

Clicking the flag offers an easy way to reset our calculation, and I'd be willing to bet that you tried to press the Space bar once or twice without clicking the flag first. You'll note that nothing happened. That's because the value of **count** already equaled the value of **days**.

The slider control we added to the **startAmount** monitor provides a user-friendly way to set an initial number and interact with the program. The bigger the number in **startAmount**, the bigger the final value in **newAmount** will be.

For example, if we start with four chicken feet, we would end up with 256 chicken feet after seven days. That's a lot of scratchin'.

The slider can also accept decimal values to the tenths position. To enter decimals, specify the decimal value in the min and max values of the set slider min and max control (e.g., Min: 0.1 and Max: 5.0).

Let's inspect our calculation using the single stepping feature of Scratch.

Start single stepping

We've already discussed the single stepping feature in Scratch, but single stepping through our calculations is a great way to understand the code other people have written. Essentially, you've been duplicating code at my direction, but that doesn't mean it makes sense.

Time for action – slow it down

We're going to step through the script extra slow:

1. From the **Edit** menu, select the **Set single stepping** option.

2. Then choose the **Flash blocks (slow)** menu option. In your script, the **count < days** block begins to flash.

3. Press the flag. Each block in the script that begins with the **when flag clicked** block flashes, and the monitors on the stage update accordingly.

4. Press the Space bar. Each step in the calculation flashes, and it should be slow enough that you can watch the monitors on the stage update.

5. When you've seen enough, click the **Extras** button and select the **stop single stepping** option.

Graph the values

Showing the result of our calculation in a monitor on the stage is nice, but we see only the end result. In this section, we'll graph the amount of our calculation for each day, which will provide some additional insight to the problem we're trying to solve.

Time for action – set the graph's origin

We want our graph to display in the same spot on the stage each time; therefore, we'll use the flag to reset the **double** sprite's location on the stage:

1. From the **Motion** palette, add the **go to x and y** block to the end of the existing **when flag clicked** script. Enter **-200** for the **x value** and **-140** for the **y value**.

2. When we reset the sprite's coordinates, we also want to clear any graphs we may have drawn. From the **Pen** palette, add the **clear** block.

3. Click the flag to position the **double** sprite to the bottom-left corner of the stage.

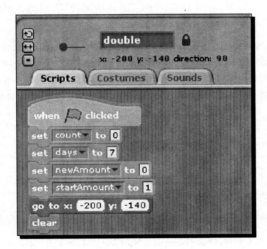

What just happened?

By now, you should be able to tell me what just happened with the blocks we added. This code was relatively simple. We sent our sprites to a specific starting point on the stage when the flag was clicked.

The **clear** block is new and will clear any graphs we draw with the pen tool. We'll cover the pen tool in the next exercise.

Time for action – draw a graph

We want to graph each day and newAmount pair in our calculation. To help accomplish this task, we'll add a **broadcast** block to the end of the **forever if** block.

1. With the **double** sprite selected, add a **broadcast** block as the last block in the **forever if** block. Add a second **broadcast** block before the **forever if** block starts so that we make sure we graph day 1.

2. Create a new broadcast message named **graph**, and select it in both **broadcast** blocks.

3. For every broadcast we send, we need to program something to receive it. From the **Control** palette, add a **when I receive** block to the **double** sprite. Make sure **graph** is set in the drop-down menu.

4. In our graph, **days** will be represented by an **x value** and the **newAmount** will be represented by a **y value**. From the **Motion** palette, add a **change y by** block and a **change x by** block.

5. We'll let each day represent ten pixels on our Scratch stage, so enter the number **10** as the value of the **change x by** block.

6. For the **y value**, we need a way to limit the height of our graph, so we're going to conduct a calculation on the **newAmount** value before we graph it. From the **Operators** palette, add the **mathematical functions** block. This block displays the **sqrt** function by default, as seen in the following screenshot:

7. From the drop-down list in the **mathematical functions** block, choose the natural logarithm notation, **ln**.

8. Add the **newAmount** variable to the input of the **mathematical functions** block.

9. Add the **stamp** block to the **change x by** block. The following screen shot shows what our scripts look like for the double sprite.

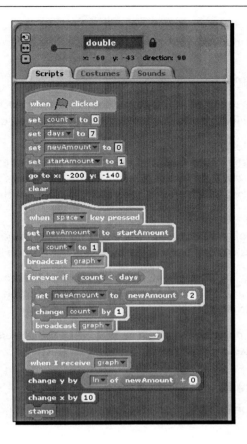

10. Press the Space bar to draw a graph.

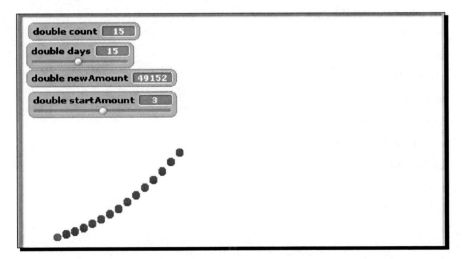

Experiment with setting different values for **startAmount** and **days** and observe the graph. Depending on the values you use, your graph may look a little different than my screenshot.

What just happened?

You did look at the values reported in the **newAmount** monitor block, didn't you? If I gave you three pesos and doubled it every day for the next 15 days, you'd end up with 49,152 pesos. Wow.

We used a few tricks to graph each **days** and **newAmount** pair. For each day in our calculation, we moved to the right by ten pixels. This number works because we will never calculate more than 30 days, which means, we need 300 pixels on the X axis to draw our biggest graph.

The Y axis presented a problem because of the larger numbers assigned to the **newAmount** variable. That's why we calculated our **y value** by taking the natural log of **newAmount**.

If you calculated a value using 30 days and a **startAmount** of 5, then you realized there wasn't enough room on the stage for the last two days on our graph. For this game, we were willing to live with that.

Finally, we stamped each point on the graph so that when the **double** sprite moved to the next coordinate, we plotted a visible curve.

Mathematical functions

Scratch provides several built-in trigonometry functions to help us perform mathematical calculations:

- sqrt (square root)
- abs (absolute value)
- sin (sine)
- cos (cosine)
- tan (tangent)
- asin (arcsine)
- acos (arccosine)
- ln (natural logarithm)
- log (log base 10)
- e^ (exponential)
- 10^ (raise 10 to a power)

Create patterns with stamp

The **stamp** block in the **Pen** palette creates an impression of the sprite that remains even after the sprite changes. It can be useful to create a history of the sprite's appearance or location. Or, we can use the **stamp** block to create a pattern, like we did with our graph.

If you look at the help topic for the **stamp** block, you'll see a different example.

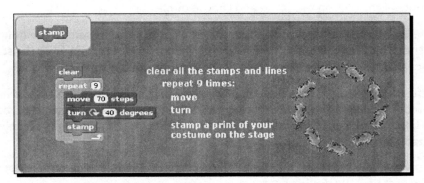

Pop quiz

1. Which of the following mathematical functions does Scratch make available for use in your scripts:
   - Square root
   - Natural logarithm
   - Cosine
   - All of the above

2. The **stamp** block does what?
   - Organizes your stamp collection
   - Chases another sprite around the stage
   - Creates a lasting impression of the sprite
   - Transforms the sprite based on a graphic effect

Connect the dots

We're going to take our graph to the next level and connect each point with a line. Let's get right to it.

Time for action – connect the dots

We need to add a new sprite and a new broadcast message to coordinate the dots with the line:

1. Duplicate the **double** sprite and name it **grapher-double**. To duplicate the **double** sprite, right-click on the sprite and choose **duplicate**.

2. When we use the duplicate option, we get a sprite with the same appearance, scripts, and variables. This time however, we don't want to carry over the scripts or variables, so delete them all from the **grapher-double** sprite.

3. After we draw a point on the graph, we need to connect the line. Create a new broadcast message to make this happen. With the **double** sprite selected, add a **broadcast** block to the end of the script that begins with the **when I receive graph** block.

4. Create a new broadcast message named **connect**. The following screenshot shows the script for the **double** sprite:

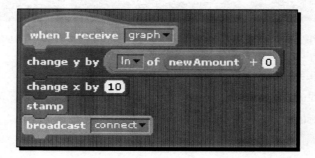

5. Now, we need to program the **grapher-double** sprite to act on the broadcast message. Add the **when I receive** block to the **double** sprite's script area. Select **connect** from the drop-down menu.

6. The **grapher-double** sprite will chase the **double** sprite across the screen. From the **Motion** palette, add the **go to** block to the **when I receive** block. From the drop-down list, select the **double** sprite.

7. As the **grapher-double** sprite chases the **double** sprite, we want to draw a line. From the **Pen** palette, add the **pen down** block to the **go to** block. From the **Pen** palette, add the **set pen size to** block.

8. From the **Pen** palette, add the **set pen color to** block to the **set pen size to** block.

9. From the **Pen** palette, add the **pen down** block to the **set pen color to** block.

10. Run the script. Click the **flag** to reset the values, and then press the Space bar. The points on the graph should be connected by a line.

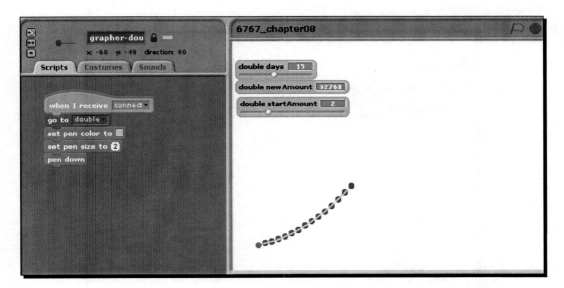

If you didn't adjust your pen size and color, feel free to customize those values. A larger pen size creates a thicker line.

When you click on the color square in the **set color** block, a color palette displays. Set the color by picking a spot with the eye dropper.

What just happened?

Calculate—Graph—Draw. These are the three general tasks in our project to this point.

Each time the **double** sprite calculated a value for the **newAmount** variable, it broadcast the graph message, which signaled the **double** sprite to move to a set of coordinates where it created a dot with the **stamp** block. After the **double** sprite created a dot, the **grapher-double** sprite chased after the **double** sprite, leaving a line in its wake.

When we clicked the flag, our graph was cleared from the stage. That's because we added the **clear** block to the double block in one of our earlier exercises.

Our graph almost worked correctly. If you studied the line we just added with the pen tool, you noticed that the line probably didn't start until the third dot or so. If you tested different **days** and **startAmount** values, then you might have seen an errant line, as shown in the following screenshot:

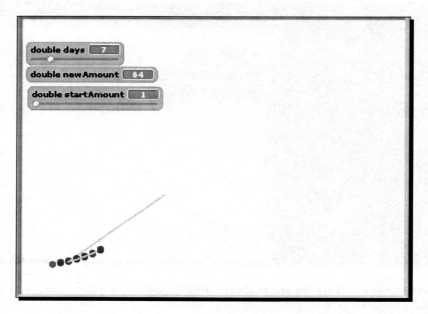

Before we fix this problem, see if you can identify why our line doesn't draw like we expect, and see if you can come up with a solution. I'll wait.

Time for action – fix the graph

Did you fix the graph? We need to reset the position of the **grapher-double** sprite to the graph's origin when we click the flag:

1. With the **grapher-double** sprite selected, add a **when flag clicked** block to the scripts area.

2. Add the **go to x: and y:** block.

3. Set the **x value** to **-200** and the **y value** to **-140**.

4. Add the clear block from the Pen palette to clear the lines that connects the dots when the flag is clicked.

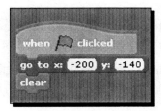

5. Click the flag and run the program by pressing the Space bar.

6. Repeat as many times as you want with several different starting values.

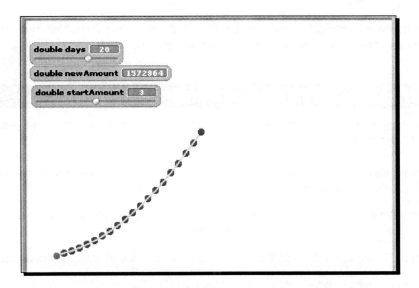

That looks a lot better. Now, let's review some of the important blocks that make our graph work.

Follow a sprite with the go to block

The **go to** block warrants some scrutiny. As we saw with our exercise, we can use the **go to** block to make one sprite go to the location of another sprite. What we do as the sprite moves is up to our imagination. For example, we could apply graphical effects; use the pen tool to draw a design, or any a number of things.

If we look at the drop-down list in the **go to** block, we'll note that all the sprites in our project are listed except the currently selected sprite. It doesn't make sense to direct a sprite to go to itself.

We can also set a sprite to go to the position of the mouse cursor, which means we could control the movement of a sprite on the stage by moving the mouse.

There are many sample Scratch projects that make a sprite chase after the mouse cursor.

Draw with the pen tool

By applying effects, such as size, color, and shading with the **pen down** block, we can trace a pattern with the sprite. When we want to stop tracing the sprite's movement, we use the **pen up** block. This is different from the **stamp** block, which creates an impression of the sprite at any given time.

The blocks in the **pen** palette provide a great way to draw dynamic patterns, such as a kaleidoscope, fireworks, line art, and many other imaginative objects.

Time for action – draw the x and y axis of the grid

Right now, the graph looks out of place. Let's draw some reference points to the graph starting with the X and Y axes:

1. Use the **paint new sprite** option to draw a small square sprite, and name it **grid**. You can use any color you want, but I'm using black.

2. Let's draw the X axis first. From the **Motion** palette, add the **go to x: and y:** block. Set our original X and Y coordinates **(-200, -140)**.

3. From the **Pen** palette, add the **set pen color to** block and select **black** as the color.

4. From the **pen** palette, add the **pen down** block.

5. From the **Motion** palette, add the **change x by** block and set the value to **320**. We'll build the graph 20 pixels bigger than we expect to use.

6. From the **Pen** palette, add the **pen up** block.

7. Next, we need to draw the Y axis. We can use the same block of code with a couple of slight alterations. Duplicate the existing blocks and append it to the script.

8. Since we want to draw the Y axis, we need to swap out the second **change x by** block with a **change y by** block.

9. Set the value in the **change y by** block to **300**.

10. After we draw the line, we don't want to see the **grid** sprite any longer. From the **Looks** palette, add the **hide** block to the end of the script.

11. Double-click on the script and draw the grid.

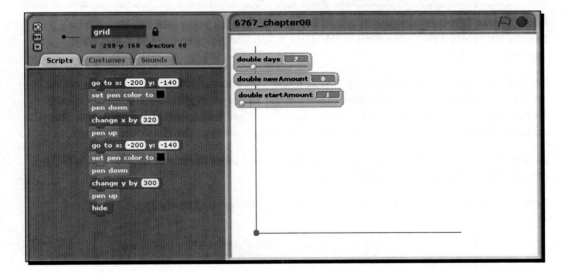

At this point, we need to decide how we want to control the **grid** sprite because after we click the flag, our grid will disappear. I'm going to choose to add a **when space key pressed** control block to the top of my script so that it is consistent with the previous sprites. And the less controls our program uses, the easier it will be to use.

What just happened?

Using one sprite, we drew two lines that only touched at the origin of our graph. After the **grid** sprite drew for 320 pixels, we applied the **pen up** block. This prevented any additional marks on the screen.

To draw the Y axis, we went back to the graph's origin, put the pen tool down, and drew a vertical line for 300 pixels.

Our numbers were not totally random. We changed x by 320 because we needed at least 300 pixels for a 30-day graph. Remember, we set one day equal to ten pixels in our original graphing formula.

The 300 pixels on the Y axis got us to the top of the stage without going off the edge. Even though our graph could potentially go off the stage, keeping our Y axis just short of the stage edge helps reinforce an off-the-charts reaction when we get really big numbers.

Have a go hero

Adding some labels to our graphs would be nice. Before we jump into the formula to calculate interest, take some time to label our graph. I'm going to call the X axis Days and the Y axis Amt.

Next, identify days 15 and 30 on the X axis. If you like, you can try to identify some major numbers on the Y axis, but the calculations we use to graph might create some problems identifying label points. Remember, this graph accurately represents the data with a sharp, upward trending curve rather than a precise representation of the data on the graph.

Because this graph won't be permanent, set each new label to hide when the flag is clicked and to show when the space key is pressed.

Review the following screenshot if you need some help getting started:

 Each label is a sprite you create with the Text tool in the Paint Editor.

Label the newAmount value

Even if we do find some way to accurately label some points on the Y axis, our graph will be representing very large numbers. It will help our user to understand the problem better if we label the final value in our calculation.

Let's add an **if** block to the **grapher-double** sprite to say the final amount.

Time for action – label newAmount

We will once again compare the **days** and **count** values as a way to determine if we should perform an action. This time, we want to know when to display the value in the **newAmount** variable:

1. Select the **double** sprite from the list of sprites.

2. Add a second **when space key pressed** control block to the scripts area.

3. Add a **wait until** block to the **when space key pressed** block.

4. We want to wait until count = days before we run our code. Add the = block to the **wait until** block.

5. From the **Variables** palette, add the **count** block to the left side of the **equals** block and the **days** block to the right side of the equals block.

6. From the **Looks** palette, add the **say** block to the **wait until** block.

7. We want to report the value in the **newAmount** variable, so drag the **newAmount** block into the **say** block.

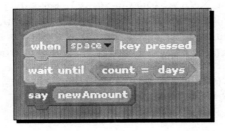

8. Run the script. The final value displays in a speech bubble on the screen.

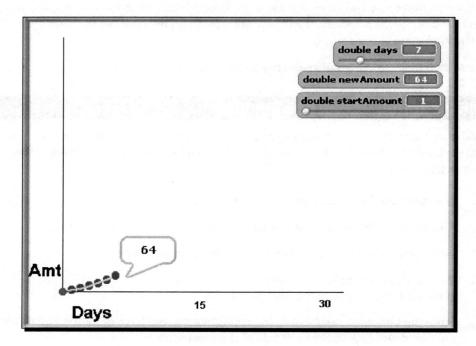

What just happened?

If we started with one dog bone and doubled it every day for seven days, we would have ended up with 64 dog bones. Our Scratch program told us so. Our dog would love us.

When the **count** equaled the **days**, we told our sprite to say whatever amount was in the **newAmount** variable. Because the **newAmount** variable constantly changed throughout the program, the only calculated value we cared about was the last one. We knew we had the last calculated value when **count < days** no longer evaluated to true.

The first scenario to cause **count** not to be less than **days** was when **count** was equal to **days**, which was the logic we represented in our script.

Pop quiz

1. The **go to** block can do all of the following except:
   ◆ Go to the location of another sprite
   ◆ Go to location of the mouse cursor
   ◆ Go to the location of the current sprite

2. Which of the following effects can you set via the **Pen** palette:

   ◆ Color
   ◆ Shading
   ◆ Size
   ◆ All of the above

Find the interest earned on a lump sum

We're finally ready to move on to the second piece of our problem. We now know how rapidly a single dollar can grow if we double it each day. For comparison, we're going to assume we have a lump sum of $15,000 that will accrue interest over a single time period, which we'll assume is 30 days.

We'll allow the user to set the interest rate. Instead of graphing this equation, we'll add a wise old sprite to do the math for us and report the total amount for comparison with the double graph.

Time for action – calculate interest on lump sum

For this calculation, we will allow the user to set the interest rate, but we'll assume a static starting amount of $15,000. You decide whether or not you want to calculate dollars, candy bars, pine cones, or something else entirely.

The formula to calculate simple interest is:

Interest Earned = Principal Amount * Interest Rate * Time

1. Add a new sprite to the stage. Feel free to choose any sprite you want, but I'm going to select the fantasy13 sprite from the d folder. Name the sprite **Lump**, as in lump sum.

2. Create three new for this sprite only variables for the **Lump** sprite, named **lumpSum**, **interestEarned**, and **interestRate**.

3. Build the calculation for the **Lump** sprite. Add the **when key pressed** block to the **Lump** sprite's script area. Select the **up arrow** from the drop-down list.

4. From the **Variables** palette, add the **set to** block to the **when key pressed** block. Select **interestEarned** from the variables list.

5. First, calculate the interest on 15,000 for a time interval of 1 month. Add the **multiplication** block from the **Operators** palette to the **set to** block. Type **15000** in the first field of the **multiplication** block. This is our principal amount.

6. Add another **multiplication** block to the second field of the first **multiplication** block.

7. Type the number **1** in the second field of the **multiplication** block you just added. This is the value for the time interval.

8. We need to turn the interest rate into a decimal value before we use it in our equation. Add a **division** block to the first field of the **multiplication** block. Type **100** as the divisor (the second field in the **division** block).

9. From the **Variables** palette, add the **interestRate** block as the dividend.

10. Now that we have the interest earned, we need to add it to the principal amount. Add a **set to** block to the end of the script. Select **lumpSum** from the list of variables.

11. Add an **addition** block to the **set to** block. Type **15000** in the first field. Add the **interestEarned** block to the second field.

12. Press the up arrow to calculate the interest in our equation. If you look at the **lumpSum** monitor on the stage, it reports **15000** because we calculated a zero percent interest by default.

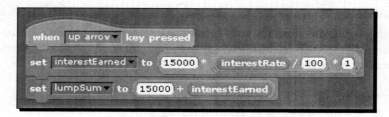

What just happened?

Mathematically speaking, there was nothing complex about this calculation. We divided the interest by 100 to convert the interest rate into a decimal value, which we then multiplied by our time interval of 1. Finally, we multiplied that amount by our starting amount, 15000, to get the total interest we earned.

We determined the final amount by adding the interest earned to the principal amount.

If you wanted to, you could have set up variables for the principal amount and the time interval. I chose to keep things simple in this calculation for demonstration purposes.

Have a go hero

Set some limits on the interestRate variable so that users can enter only a range, such as 0.1 to 10.0. Allow the user to set the interest rate via the slider.

After you set the min and max slider values for the interestRate variable, make the sprite say the lumpSum amount.

Run the script multiple times to test it out.

Round to nearest whole number

The interest calculation produces numbers to the nearest one hundredth value, as in 15602.59. There's nothing wrong with that, but since our other calculation reports whole numbers, we should be consistent and round off to the nearest whole number.

The **Operators** palette contains a **round** block that we can apply to any number. The following screenshot shows two acceptable ways to implement the **round** block in the context of the previous exercise:

Standard rounding rules apply. Values of .5 and higher will round up to the next whole number. For example, 6.5 becomes 7. Values less than .5 will round down to the nearest whole number. For example, 6.4 becomes 6.

Have a go hero

We have a reasonably complete program that compares two possible ways to accumulate money, but it needs some finishing touches. This hero exercise asks you to add those finishing touches:

◆ Add a **directions** sprite to the stage that asks the user for an answer to the following problem: Would you rather earn 4% interest on $15,000 for one month or receive $1 that doubles every day for 15 days?

◆ Change the **Lump** sprite to use a broadcast message as the control to calculate the interest amount instead of the up arrow.

◆ Add a control to reset the interestRate variable on the **Lump** sprite when the flag is set.

◆ Document some instructions in the project notes field.

The list could be endless. Feel free to customize this as you see fit.

Next steps

This project spawns a lot of related ideas. You could build on the existing project by creating an interactive math lesson that asks a user to choose a starting number. Then, calculate the results and explain the math behind the results. After that, prompt for user-selected values.

You could use the **stamp** block to fill up the stage with grains of rice to show the power of doubling.

Our formula used a simple interest calculation, but you could apply the same principles we learned in this chapter to build a project to calculate and graph compound interest.

Of course, you could also create a project that illustrates mathematical folktales.

Using the pen tool in conjunction with the mathematical functions, you can create elaborate interactive art projects. Our project created a simple graph, but stop by the Pen Gallery on the Scratch web site for some inspiration: `http://scratch.mit.edu/galleries/view/24716`.

Summary

Not only did we use math to solve our question, but we also learned that doubling is a very powerful concept when applied over time. Double my money, please!

With the exception of the pen tool and the mathematical functions, this chapter built on many of the concepts we've learned before. Specifically, we relied heavily on the use of variables to provide an interactive project that is capable of crunching a wide range of number combinations.

This chapter introduced mathematical functions and the pen tool to help us play out the action on the stage. We used math to solve three types of problems in our program. First, we solved the equations. Second, we used math as a conditional check to determine if we needed to double our amount one more time. Third, we used a trigonometric function to graph the results of the double equation in a way that scaled to the Scratch stage.

Much like in daily life, we can't escape math as Scratch programmers. This knowledge is worth accumulating and, once we have it, we can turn the math into a visual message using Scratch's other programming capabilities, including the pen tool, to create designs.

We've covered Scratch's major functionalities, and in the event I've missed something, you have all the information you need to discover it on your own.

Now, we will go forth and share our projects with the world.

9
Share!

Imagine. Program. Share. We have been working hard programming our imagination, but now it's time to share our creativity with the world. Sharing not only lets us show off our work, but it also gives us an opportunity to receive feedback that we can then use to improve our projects.

Now that we have projects in our portfolio, it's time to share them with a wider audience. In this chapter, we will:

- ◆ *Share our projects with the Scratch community*
- ◆ *Use social networks to promote our projects*
- ◆ *Host projects on our own web site*

Come on. Let's not keep our work a secret.

Share with the Scratch community

As you browse projects on the Scratch web site, you may notice some projects get featured while, others have a lot of views and "love its." As a new Scratch programmer, we need to focus on developing our programming skills rather than trying to win a popularity contest.

Don't get discouraged if your projects seem to get lost among the thousands of other community projects. You'll eventually find an audience with the help of this chapter.

Now, let's select a project to share. I'm going to use the pong project from Chapter 6.

Reduce file size

When we share our work on the Web, we need to be conscious of how big our project file gets. Images and sounds will increase our file size more than anything else, and projects with large files take longer to load and play from the Web.

Fortunately, Scratch gives us a way to reduce the file size of our images and sounds before we share them on the Web.

Time for action – compress media files

Before we share our work, let's make our project as small as possible:

1. First, compress the images in the project. From the Edit menu, select the **Compress images** option to display the **JPEG Quality** dialog box.

2. Set a quality number between 0 and 100. In my example, I'll use 80.

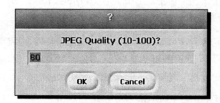

 Choosing a higher JPEG quality creates a clearer image, but it also creates a bigger file size.

3. Click **OK** to have Scratch compress any JPEG images. When finished, Scratch will report the number of images it compressed. Click **OK** to accept the message.

4. Next, compress the sounds. From the **Edit** menu, select **compress sounds** to display a list of compression options.

5. Select the sound quality you want and click **OK**. **Normal** should work in most cases.

 Higher quality settings create the best sound quality, but it also creates a bigger file size.

6. When finished, Scratch displays the number of sounds it compressed. Click **OK** to accept the message.

What just happened?

When we share our projects on the Web, we want to make our project as small as possible so that people can play our games, watch our stories, and experience our animations in a friendly way.

Hopefully, we will have chosen values that provide an acceptable level of quality for our media while enabling a positive experience for our users.

Share!

If you want your Scratch project to display a certain way, make sure you set the stage before you share the project. For example, if you need certain sprites to be hidden when the game loads, hide the sprites before you share the project because Scratch will remember its state.

Time for action – share!

Let's share our work:

1. From the **Edit** menu, select the **Share This Project Online** option to display the **Upload to server** dialog box.

2. Enter the requested information. Most of it should be self-explanatory, such as Your Scratch web site login name, Password, Project name, and Project notes.

 We created a login to the Scratch web site in Chapter 3. If you did not create a username and password, then click the **Create account** link.

3. Scratch allows us to label our projects with tags. Select the tags that best describe the project. I'm sharing pong, so I'll label my project as a game.

4. Type additional tags to identify the project if necessary. These can be anything you like. I'm going to enter pong as a tag.

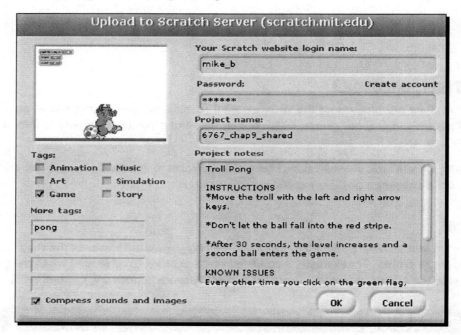

5. Click **OK** to upload the project to the Scratch web site. A status message displays while the project uploads.

6. When the project upload completes, an **Upload Succeeded** message displays. Click **OK** to accept the message.

You can now view your project online. Go to `http://scratch.mit.edu` in your web browser, and look for your project in the **Newest Projects** category.

If, for some reason, you're unable to find your project on the front page of the Newest Projects gallery, then log in to your Scratch account to display your project list. Click on the project to play it online.

What just happened?

Congratulations! You contributed your first project to the Scratch community with the click of a button.

Prior to uploading the project, we were prompted to describe our project with information, including the title, a description, and the tags. The information we entered will help our projects be found on the Scratch web site.

Tag it

It seems like every site we visit uses a tagging system as a user-defined classification system. Scratch is no exception.

The problem with most tagging systems is that they rely entirely on user-entered data, which means tags are duped and inconsistently used. For example, I may use the "game" tag one time and the "games" tag another time. Because our goal is to quickly label and identify items with tags, this is a problem.

Scratch helps us out a little bit by providing several default tags for Animation, Art, Game, Music, Simulation, and Story. By selecting one or more of these broad categories, we begin to consistently label our projects.

We're able to refine our description with user-specified tags. So, if our game happens to be about fishing, we could specify "fishing" as a tag. If your project promotes an ideal or argues for a position on an issue, you could use the "propaganda" tag. Just checking to see how closely you're reading. Anything goes as a tag.

On the Scratch web site, we can browse popular tags via the tag cloud. The following screenshot shows a tag cloud from the Scratch web site:

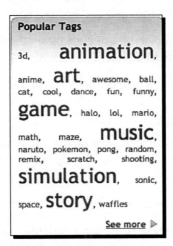

The most popular tags are represented with a large font size and are bold. Notice any similarities between the tag cloud and the default tags in the share dialog? The most popular tags on the web site are also the default tags. Click on any tag to browse all projects associated with that tag.

Update a project

It's likely that you will change a project after you've uploaded it to the Scratch web site, and you will want to update the version of the project on the web site. However, Scratch doesn't have an update button.

So, what do you do?

Share the project using the **Share!** button. When prompted for a **Program Name**, enter the same name that you used the first time you shared the program. This will update your project on the Scratch web site.

In order to view the updated project on the Scratch web site, you may need to clear your Java cache. On Windows, right-click on the **java** icon in the system tray and select the **open console** option. Type **x** to clear the cache.

Close the console and view your project again. Don't forget to refresh the page in your browser.

Trouble?

There are a couple of problems that may pop up when you share your project on the Web. Let's take a look at two issues, as of Scratch 1.3.1.

Firefox display problems

If you're a Firefox user, then the Scratch application may be too small when you view it on the Scratch web site. For example, the right and bottom edges of the stage will not be visible.

To work around this problem, zoom in on the page by simultaneously pressing the **Ctrl** and **+** keys until the stage is fully visible.

Alternatively, you can resize the page by selecting **View | Zoom | Zoom In** from Firefox's menu.

Variables change positions

You may experience a problem with a variable on the stage reverting to its original position on the stage. For example, the variable may move from the center of the stage to the top-left corner.

This is a known issue with a workaround.

Before you upload your project, make sure all the variables are visible on the stage. Then, create a script that hides the variable when the flag is clicked.

Save the project and upload it.

Link to your project

Tags make it easy for other users to find our project, but there's a lot of competition for views on the site. To promote our projects, we may choose to link to them from our own web site.

Scratch provides the HTML snippets to embed the project as an image or a Java applet on our web site in the same way you embed YouTube videos.

Whether you have a Joomla!, Moodle, or regular web page, you can embed your Scratch project; we embed a project the same way. We add the HTML snippet from the Scratch web site into the HTML code of our web page. All content management systems or blogs provide a way to do this. Consult your documentation for assistance.

I'll demonstrate the process using a WordPress blog post. Even if you don't have WordPress, you'll be able to follow along for most of the process.

Embed in a blog post

When we add or edit a blog post in WordPress, the default editor displays a WYSIWYG (what you see is what you get) editor. To embed the project, we need to work in the HTML view.

 If you don't have a WordPress installation or an account but want to follow along, then visit http://wordpress.com and sign up for a free blog account to promote your Scratch projects.

If you find yourself wondering what HTML means, then you probably won't feel any better to learn that it stands for Hypertext Markup Language. It's the code that tells a web browser what to display when you visit a web page.

Fortunately, you can perform this task without any real knowledge of HTML. Knowing how to copy and paste will get the job done.

Open your game on the Scratch web site and scroll down the page until you see the heading **Link to this Project**. Click the **Embed** link to display the HTML snippets that you need to copy into your blog post.

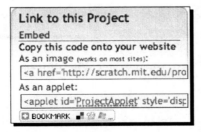

Copy either the image or the applet code, and paste it into the HTML view of the blog's post editor. Click on the **HTML** tab to see the post's code view. See the following screenshot for an example using WordPress:

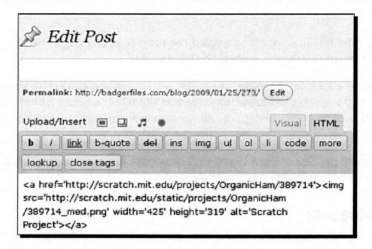

Embed an applet or an image?

If we embed the Java applet into our blog post, then users will be able to play the game without leaving our site. The following screenshot shows a Java applet embedded in a blog post at my site, `http://www.badgerfiles.com`.

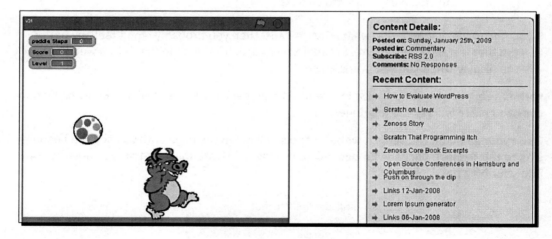

Note that with the applet, we have the flag and stop controls.

If we embed our project as an image, then our post displays as a link that takes the user to the Scratch web site to play the game. The following screenshot shows what the embedded image looks like:

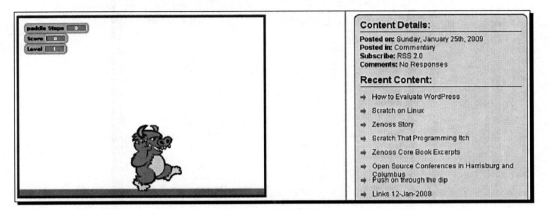

The embedded image does not display the flag and stop controls.

How you decide which method to use is a matter of preference. Do you want to keep visitors on your site or send them to the Scratch web site? Embedding the Java applet keeps visitors on your site.

There is a technical consideration that may make the choice easy. Not everyone will be able to embed a Java applet. Some web hosts, such as the free **wordpress.com** accounts, do not allow users to embed Java applets. Therefore, embedding an image is the only option.

Share via social networks

Want to share your project on Delicious, Facebook, Digg, Twitter, MySpace, Slashdot, or any other popular social network site? No problem. Each project page contains an **AddThis.com** button that's also listed under the **Link to this Project** section.

To share a project, hover the mouse over the **BOOKMARK** button to display a list of popular sites.

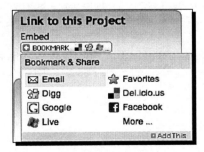

If you don't see the network you want, click on the **More...** button to display a new window of options.

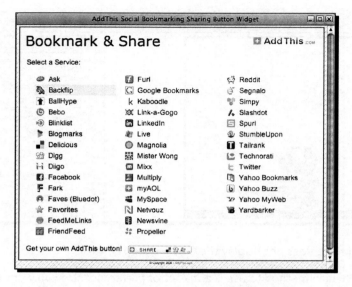

To share your project, click on the service name. The **AddThis.com** widget will prompt you for a username and password so that it can log in to the service and post the project link to your profile.

Presumably, we already have friends, connections, and followers on our social networks. Therefore, adding our Scratch project is one way we can attract views, comments, and fans to our creative works.

Subscribe to projects via RSS

Another way you can cultivate viewers is to entice other people to subscribe to the Really Simple Syndication (RSS) feed of your projects. An RSS feed notifies subscribers when you post a new project.

 The best way to learn about RSS is to use it. Start with this Common Craft video: http://www.commoncraft.com/rss_plain_english.

There are numerous RSS readers available, but Google Reader is a popular example. You can learn more at http://www.google.com/reader. Firefox also contains a built-in RSS reader called Live Bookmarks.

Expecting to attract RSS subscribers as a new Scratch programmer may not be realistic, but computer clubs or organizations can use RSS as a way for members to receive automatic project notifications from other members.

How to subscribe

A user's page in Scratch displays a list of projects with a **Subscribe** link. If you visit my user page at `http://scratch.mit.edu/users/mike_b`, you will see a list of all the projects that we've created in this book.

When you click on the **Subscribe** link, how your computer interprets the content will depend on how your computer reads RSS feeds. In most cases, you will be prompted to add the feed to your RSS reader.

In worst-case scenarios, the content of the feed will display and you will need to manually add the URL of the feed to an RSS reader. The following screenshot shows the RSS feed for my recent projects, as seen from the Mozilla Firefox web browser:

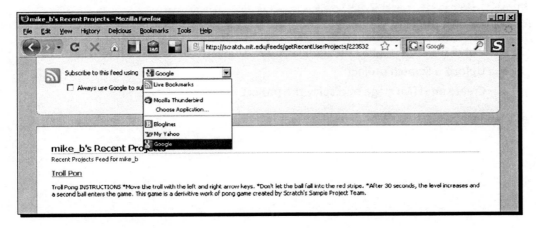

I'd like to point out a few items. In the browser's address bar is the URL of my project feed: `http://scratch.mit.edu/feeds/getRecentUserProjects/223532`. You can paste this URL into any RSS reader and gain instant access to my projects' feeds without visiting the Scratch web site.

Next is a **Subscribe to this feed using** drop-down list that contains a few RSS readers. I use Google, so that's the one I selected from the list. After you click on the application to read your feed, click on the **Subscribe** link, which is currently obstructed by the drop-down list in the screenshot.

Go ahead, give it a try.

Host your Scratch projects

The Scratch web site is easy and it likely meets the needs of most people, but we're not limited to hosting our projects on the Scratch web site. We can use our own web servers.

There are several reasons to self-host our Scratch projects. Your classroom or community center may have limited access or bandwidth, which makes uploading and viewing projects on the Web difficult. You might prefer to keep the projects private or not allow others to remix the content. Or, you might simply want to build web site traffic to your own web site. Regardless of the reason, we can do it.

This is a relatively advanced topic for our book, and I'll assume you know something about FTP and web servers to complete this section. More importantly, it requires you to have access to a web server.

Install files to a web server

To host our own projects, we need to complete the following tasks:

- ◆ Install the Java support files, which are available from the Scratch web site
- ◆ Upload a Scratch project
- ◆ Create an HTML page to display the project

Let's begin.

Time for action – install files on a web server

1. Download these two files from the Scratch web site and save them to your computer:
   1. `http://scratch.mit.edu/static/misc/ScratchApplet.jar`
   2. `http://scratch.mit.edu/static/misc/soundbank.gm`

> If your web browser displays the contents of the `soundbank.gm` file in the browser, use the browser's File | Save Page As... feature to save it to a file on your computer.

2. Create a directory on the web server. I'm going to create a directory named `scratch` in the web server's root directory.

3. Upload the `ScratchApplet.jar` and `soundbank.gm` files to the directory you just created on the web server.

4. Upload a Scratch project to the scratch directory you created on the web server.

5. Now, we need to build an HTML page to display the project. Save the following code as `scratch.html`:

```
<html>
<title>Mike's Scratch Project</title>
<body>
<applet id="ProjectApplet" style="display:block"
code="ScratchApplet" codebase="./" archive="ScratchApplet.jar"
height="387" width="482"> <param name="project" value="project-
name.sb">
</applet>
</body>
</html>
```

6. In the `scratch.html` code, find the **value** attribute and change `project-name.sb` to the filename of the project you uploaded to the web server.

7. Upload `scratch.html` to the scratch directory on your web server. The following screenshot shows my FTP server on the right and the contents of the scratch directory:

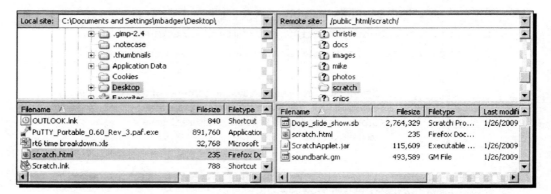

8. Open a web browser and view the URL of the page you created. In my example, that page is `http://badgerfiles.com/scratch/scratch.html`.

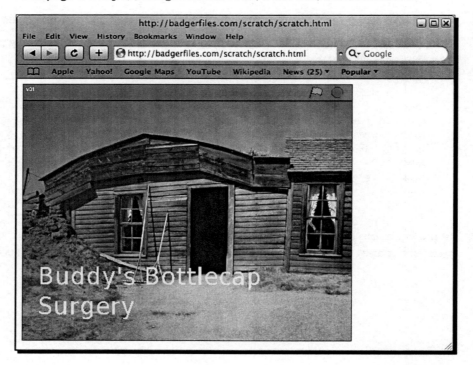

We're now hosting our own Scratch projects.

What just happened?

With just a bit of knowledge about how the Web works, we were able to host our own Scratch projects. The files we downloaded from the Scratch web site enabled our projects to run as a Java applet, just like they do on the Scratch web site. We mixed in a bit of HTML in order to display the project in a browser.

If you compared the HTML code we created with the HTML snippet we embedded into the blog post earlier in the chapter, then you realized they were the same code with a few accommodations. The paths to the projects varied and our exercise created a full HTML page, whereas the snippet was only the project code.

Limitations of self-hosting

Beyond the obvious limitations like needing a web server, self-hosting your Scratch projects means you don't have the same tools that the Scratch web site provides, such as built-in social network promotion.

Also, no project notes display by default. This means that if a visitor comes to our Scratch page, they may not know how to play our game unless we manually add the notes as part of the HTML page.

Pop quiz

1. Why should you want to compress images and sounds before sharing a project?

    ❑   To combine multiple files into one file

    ❑   To decrease the quality of the images and sounds

    ❑   To make the images and sounds smaller

    ❑   You never want to compress images or sounds

2. If you want to update a Scratch project that you previously shared, what do you do?

    ❑   Click the **Update!** button in the Scratch interface

    ❑   Delete the project from your account on the Scratch web site and share the revised project

    ❑   You are not able to update the project

    ❑   Share the project using the **Share!** button in the Scratch interface and use the same name as the original project

3. What are the ways in which you can share your projects with the world?

- ❑ Post your project to social networks, such as Facebook, MySpace, and Twitter using the AddThis.com bookmarks on the Scratch web site
- ❑ Embed the project link in a web site
- ❑ Self-host your Scratch projects on your own web server
- ❑ All of the above

Summary

We've learned everything we need to know to show off our Scratch programming skills to the world. Scratch makes sharing easy via the Scratch web site and includes several built-in ways to promote your projects on your web site or social networks.

For the do-it-yourself types, self-hosting Scratch projects on our web server is a snap. We have no excuses for keeping our projects hidden on our hard drives.

In the next chapter, we'll experiment with the PicoBoard from Playful Invention Company to see if we can use real-world stimuli to control our Scratch projects.

10
Real-world stimuli

Scratch enables you to incorporate real-world information into your projects using webcams and sensory boards known as PicoBoards. The webcam support allows us to import pictures as costumes and backgrounds for inclusion into our projects.

Stimulate your sprites with real-world sensory data by connecting a PicoBoard from Playful Invention Company to the USB port on a Windows or Macintosh computer. The board provides several sensors that turn sound, light, motion, touch, and electrical resistance into inputs that we can use to animate our projects.

In this chapter, we will:

◆ *Import pictures with a webcam*

◆ *Install a PicoBoard*

◆ *Make Scratch respond to motion, sound, touch, light, and electrical resistance*

Let's bring the outside world to our projects.

Import webcam pictures

Have a webcam connected to your computer? Starting with Scratch 1.4, you can import still pictures from your webcam into your Scratch projects.

Time for action – say cheese

Plug your webcam in because we're going to take a self portrait.

1. Open a new Scratch project.

2. Click on the **Costumes** tab.

3. Click on the **Camera** button to display a real-time view from your webcam.

4. When you get the shot you want, click the button with a picture of a camera on it.

5. Click **Done** to close the camera window.

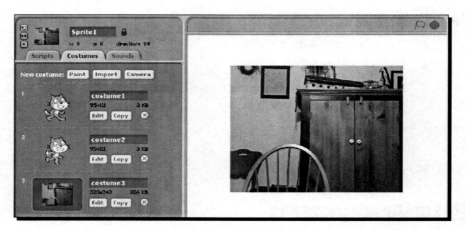

What just happened?

As long as the webcam was working correctly with your computer, Scratch automatically detected the camera and made the images available to us. Each time we clicked the camera button, Scratch imported the current picture as a 320 x 240 pixel costume.

Using the webcam, we can also import backgrounds by selecting the **stage** before opening the camera. When importing a background image, Scratch automatically resizes the image to the size of the stage (480 x 360 pixels).

Working with camera images

After we import pictures from the webcam, we can work with the images just like we would any other sprite, costume, or background. We can manipulate the images using the same concepts we've used throughout this book, including editing the images in the Paint Editor.

 Right click on the image of the sprite from the stage to get several editing options: resize, rotate, export, duplicate, delete, and grab a screen region to create a new sprite.

Many of the sprites include costume variations by default, as we see with the Scratch cat. Using the camera feature, you could import several variations of a scene or portrait, such as different expressions: happy, sad, and scowl. Then export the group of costumes as sprite.

Export a sprite

Have a series of camera images that you think make a sprite worth saving for use in future projects? Export it.

Right click on the sprite from the stage and choose the **export this sprite** option. Enter a filename and select a location when prompted.

You can now use the new sprite in other projects.

PicoBoard—what is it?

Not sure you want a PicoBoard? You can review the exercises in chapter to get a sense of what the board can do. Also, this chapter contains an excercise that uses gravity, which is something that will appeal to anyone who wants to make sprites fall.

With a PicoBoard, we can program our sprites to respond to real-world input from the following controls:

- Slider
- Light sensor
- Sound sensor
- Button
- Four pairs of alligator clips

What does this mean? Well, we can program a sprite to jump each time we press a button, move across the stage as we move the slider, dance when we pass in front of the light sensor, apply a graphic effect when we clap our hands, or connect the alligator clips to form a circuit. These are just some ideas to get us started.

While the PicoBoard creates a deeper connection to our projects, there is a potential downside. The projects we adapt to use with the PicoBoard can be used only while we run the projects from our computer. Projects shared on the web cannot connect to a PicoBoard.

The physical board favors function over sleek design. Measuring larger than a business card, the PicoBoard resembles something you might find on the inside of your computer. The board is not enclosed in a case; rather, the board's circuitry is exposed. It's a design that's sure to appeal to geeks of any age.

Order a PicoBoard

You need to order the PicoBoard directly from the Playful Invention Company web site at `www.picocricket.com/picoboard.html`.

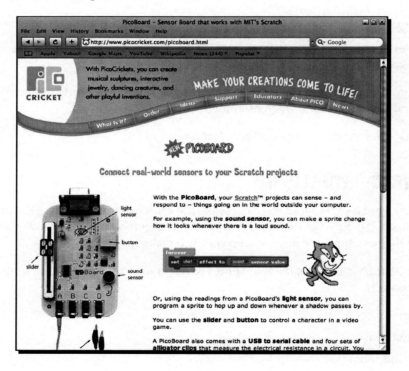

At the time of this writing, the board cost $50 USD plus shipping and handling charges. Delivery will take up to four weeks. You should always check with the Playful Invention Company for current prices and shipping information.

Install the PicoBoard

Congratulations on your PicoBoard purchase. As you inventory your package, make sure you have the following items:

- PicoBoard
- Serial port to USB connector
- four sets of alligator clips

Before we can start using the PicoBoard, we must ensure our computers have the proper drivers installed. The driver is just a term tech people use to sound smart, but it's really just some software we install on our computer to make the PicoBoard work properly with Scratch.

Windows Vista users can rest for a minute while the rest of us install the necessary software.

Driver installation is straightforward. Go to `www.picocricket.com/picoboardsetup.html`, and click on the download link for your operating system to download the file to your computer.

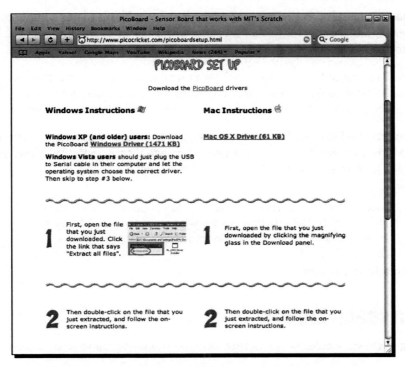

After the file downloads, unzip it using whatever tools are available on your computer. Usually, double-clicking on the file will display the contents of the ZIP file so you can extract it. Extract the setup file to your desktop and double-click it. Then, follow the installer's instructions.

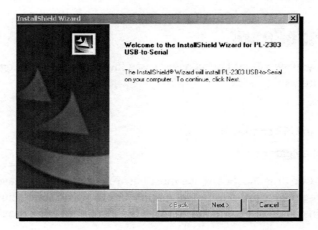

After the driver installs, connect the PicoBoard to the computer.

Connect the PicoBoard

Welcome back Vista users. We're ready to connect the PicoBoard to our computer. Find the serial port to USB connector cable that came with the PicoBoard. Connect the serial connector to the PicoBoard and the USB connector to your computer.

Not sure what a serial or USB connector is? Don't worry. The serial connector has nine pins, and the USB end looks like the connector used for your mouse, MP3 player, or printer. Computer cables plug in only one way, so find the connections that match and go for it.

After we connect the PicoBoard to the computer, the computer detects the board and makes it ready to use. Windows users will see a message display in the Windows system tray (near the clock) that indicates the new hardware is ready.

 When you work with the PicoBoard, open only one instance of Scratch. Multiple Scratch windows may cause Scratch to not detect the PicoBoard's sensor information.

Now, we're ready to program.

Capture sound input

We're going to create a quick program that switches the background when a sound is made.

Time for action – switch backgrounds on sound

Let's emulate night and day with our backgrounds so that each sound changes the scene. Open a new Scratch project and begin:

1. Create the second background by copying the default white background. Then, edit **background2** and use the fill tool to paint it black.

2. Add the **when flag clicked** control block to the scripts area of the stage.

3. Add a **forever if** block to the **when flag clicked** block.

4. We need to evaluate the sound level before we act on it. From the **Operators** palette, add the **greater than** block.

5. Now, let's evaluate the sound. From the **Sensing** palette, drag the **sensor value** block into the first field of the **greater than** block. Select the **sound** option from the drop-down list of options.

6. We want to switch the background whenever the sound is greater than 0. Type a **0** in the second field of the **greater than** block so that the statement reads **sound sensor value > 0**.

7. From the **Looks** palette, add the **next background** block to the **forever if** block.

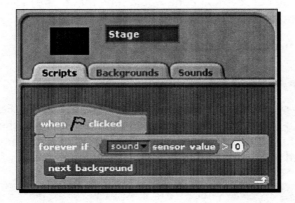

8. Click the **flag** to start the script.

9. Now clap. The background changes to black, then white, and on and on depending on how many times you clap.

10. Let's watch the sound sensor. From the **Sensing** palette, select the **sound** option in the **sensor value** block. Then click the **checkbox** next to the **sensor value** block to display the sensor value watcher on the stage.

 If you do not have a PicoBoard, do not enable the **sensor value** block, as it may lock up your Scratch program or your computer.

Let's see what effect yodeling has. If anyone hears you, just blame it on an email you received, like this: "I can't believe someone would send that to me in an email." Your background should strobe to the sound of your yodel.

Click the stop sign to make Scratch stop accepting sound input.

What just happened?

Each time we made a sound, the stage flipped between night and day. Each time the PicoBoard registered a sound, the sensor assigned a numeric value to the sound that was measured on a scale from 0 to 100. Since our script was set to act on any sound greater than 0, we didn't need to be very loud to make the backgrounds switch.

Have a go hero

Barely a whisper will make our script swap backgrounds, and that's indicative of the code we used. If the sound sensor value is greater than zero, display the next background. Use the sound sensor value monitor on the stage to find the level of your normal speech. Then, adjust your script to switch to the next background only if the sound sensor value is above the level of normal speech.

Sound as a numeric value

The PicoBoard turns the sound we make into a number from 0 to 100, where 0 represents silence. In addition to the sound sensors, the light, slider, and alligator clips use a numeric value to represent the strength of the stimulus.

Using the numeric sound value, we can perform other math functions by supplying the **sensor value** block as an input value. Think of all the other places we can use a numeric value to affect how our sprites display on the stage. The **Motion, Looks, Pen,** and **Sound** palettes all have blocks that take numeric input to transform some feature of a sprite. For example, the **move** block accepts a number as a way to control how many steps a sprite takes.

Time for action – use sound to change the sprite's looks

Let's apply some graphic effects to our sprite based on how loud of a sound we make:

1. We'll continue working with our sound script. Drag the script for the stage onto the sprite to duplicate the code.

2. Select the **cat** sprite to display the scripts area.

3. Swap out the **next costume** block with a **change effect by** block from the **Looks** palette.

4. Select an effect from the list. I'm going to use the **whirl** effect.

5. From the **Sensing** palette, drag the **sensor value** block into the input of the **change effect by** block.

6. Select the **sound** option in the **sensor value** block.

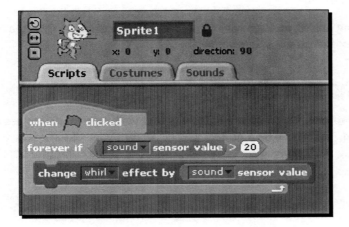

7. Now, make some noise to change the background and contort the sprite.

What just happened?

Who knew you had such a powerful voice? When you speak, sprites listen. We used one sound input to control multiple actions, but each sprite independently evaluated the sound value to determine if it should execute the code in the script or not.

Have a go hero

Grab a friend and see who has the louder voice. We've worked with variables throughout the book. Write a script that records the sound sensor value to a variable, and then configure a sprite to report the value.

Take turns making noises, and see who can score the highest value. Get creative and make the sprite jump based on the sound value.

Click for the next slide

At the end of Chapter 4, we created a slideshow that we'll now modify to use the button on the PicoBoard. This would be a perfect way to present your slideshow to a room full of friends and family, and you wouldn't need to sit in front of the computer screen to control the show.

Time for action – click for the next slide

Our original slideshow contains a **when right arrow key pressed** control block to advance the screen. We will leave that control in place so that our slideshow still works when we share it on the Web.

Open your slideshow and save it as a new project so that you can feel free to experiment without altering the original project. If you don't have the slideshow, you can download mine from this book's web site at Packt Publishing.

1. From the **Control** palette, add a **when flag clicked** block to the scripts area for the stage.

2. Add a **forever if** control block.

3. From the **Sensing** palette, add the **sensor** block as the input for the **forever if** block. Select **button pressed** from the drop-down list of options.

4. Add a **next background** block to the **forever if** block.

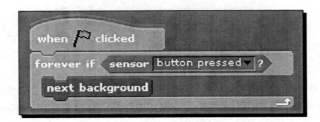

5. Now, click the button on the PicoBoard. The slideshow should have advanced, but it advanced more than one screen. Try clicking slower. Ok, don't try too hard because it's nearly impossible to guarantee we can make one button click advance only one slide at a time.

6. We can solve this timing problem with a broadcast message. From the **control** palette, add a **broadcast next and wait** block to the **forever if** block. Create a new broadcast named **next**.

7. We need to receive the broadcast, so add a **when I receive** control block to the scripts area. Select **next** as the message.

8. Move the **next background** block from the **forever if** block, and attach it to the **when I receive** block.

9. Now, try the button click again.

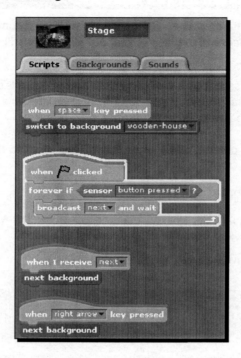

Our button clicks are a bit more controlled with the broadcast block, but the slideshow still has a tendency to advance more than one slide at a time. As you think about how we can fix the timing problem, let's examine our script.

What just happened?

Even though our script behaved a bit wonkily, we got the general idea. The PicoBoard allowed us, the slideshow narrators, to be detached from the computer screen and the keyboard. Yet, we still controlled the pace of the show.

The key to this script was the **forever if sensor button pressed** block. The sensor reported a true or false value to measure the button click. If the button was pressed (true), then we broadcast the message to switch to the next background.

True or false values

To display the value of the button pressed sensor on the stage, click on the **sensor** block from the **Sensing** palette. Each time you click on the button, the sensor reports a **true** value.

Compare this to the other PicoBoard sensors that report a range of numbers. Either the button is pressed or not; we can't measure how hard we press the button.

In addition to the button sensor, the alligator clips that connect to the A, B, C, and D sensors also report a true or false value. Later in the chapter, we'll create a project to test whether or not the alligator clips are connected.

Let's get back to our slideshow and fix our timing problem.

Time for action – wait until button not pressed

Did you come up with a way to fix our slideshow so that it advances only one screen at a time when we click the button? We're going to modify the **forever if** conditional statement to wait until the button is not pressed before continuing.

Read on for the details, but I'd love to hear other solutions, if you came up with any:

1. From the **Control** palette, add a **wait until** block to the **broadcast next** block.

2. From the **Operators** palette, add a **not** block to the **wait until** block.

3. From the **Sensing** palette, add a **sensor** block to the
   not block. Select the **button pressed** value.

4. Click the flag to reset the show. Click the button to navigate the show.

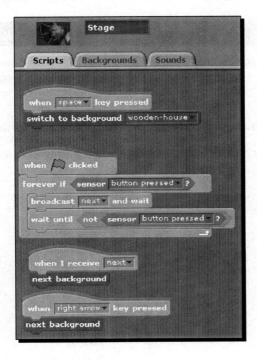

Now, that's much better. One click equals one slide.

What just happened?

To fully appreciate what just happened, let's quickly recap what we know about the **forever if** block. When the flag is clicked, the script constantly checks to see if the condition is met. The **forever if** block stops checking only when we stop the program.

In our project, the sensor value is continually evaluated. When the button pressed value equals true, the code broadcasts a message to flip to the next slide. And before the script continues, the code waits until the button pressed value equals false.

By waiting until the button was not pressed at the end of the **forever if** block, we made Scratch interpret the sensor in the way we intended: One human button click advanced the show by one slide.

Step into the light, please

While our Scratch sprites can't see the outside world, we can use the light sensor on the PicoBoard to control a sprite based on the amount of light detected by the sensor.

For this exercise, we'll modify a **dragon** sprite and make it grow based on the amount of light it receives.

Time for action

Scratch includes several sprites that have scripts by default, which means the sprite is already programmed to do something. We're going to use such a sprite to jump-start this exercise:

1.   Open a new Scratch project, and select the **choose new sprite from file** option.

2.   Open the **Fantasy** folder and select the **Growing Dragon** sprite. It's the dragon designated as having 1 script.

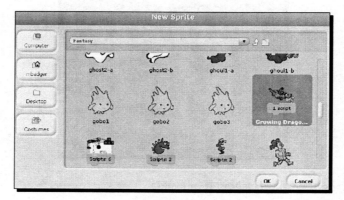

3. The sprite contains one simple script that sets the size of the dragon based on the **loudness** block. Click the **flag** and make some noise. See the dragon expand and contract.

4. Now, replace the **loudness** block that's inside the **set size to** block with the **sensor value** block. Select **light** from the drop-down list.

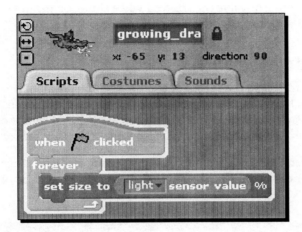

5. Enable the **light sensor** value monitor on the stage. Then, check the box to display the monitor.

6. Move the PicoBoard around the room to expose it to different concentrations of light. You can also move your finger over the light sensor.

7. As you block light or allow more light to reach the sensor, the dragon grows according to the value reported by the light sensor.

What just happened?

When we allowed more light to reach the sensor, the dragon swelled up and shot a bigger flame. As we blocked more light from reaching the sensor, the dragon became smaller, weaker, and less fierce.

The light sensor value monitor reported the amount of light the sensor detected at any given time. For example, my sensor value reported 31 while sitting on my desk. As I moved the sensor directly under a light source, the value increased.

Using light to detect motion

If we know the amount of light the sensor detects in a certain position, we can create our very own motion detector. Have you ever walked through a museum exhibit and been startled by an exhibit that started playing as you walked by? We can use the light sensor on the PicoBoard to animate our projects based on someone passing in front of the light sensor.

As an object or a person passes in front of the light sensor, less light reaches the sensor. We can use the absence of light to trigger action in our project, such as playback audio or start a presentation.

Have a go hero

Modify the control on the **Growing Dragon** sprite to activate when the PicoBoard detects motion. You'll need to know what your default light sensor value is before you can use it as a condition in your script. As you experiment, find out how close you need to pass in front of the sensor to affect your light reading.

Control motion with the slider

Next, we'll explore the slider sensor as we manipulate some gravity marbles. Like the sound and the light sensors, the slider outputs a numeric value between 0 and 100.

Let's experiment with Earth's greatest force.

Time for action – slide sensor

Like we did with the light sensor exercise, we're going to open a sprite that already has scripts associated with it. In this case, we'll use the gravity marbles.

1. Start a new Scratch project and select the **choose new sprite from file** option.
2. Delete the original sprite.

3. Open the **Things** folder and select the **Gravity Marble** sprite.

4. Click the flag and interact with the marble by pressing the arrow keys to make the marble rise and fall. Try to understand the code. When you've had enough, continue with the next step.

5. We want to raise the marble with the slider sensor on the PicoBoard. Replace the **if key up arrow pressed?** block with the **greater than** block from the **Operators** palette.

6. From the **Sensing** palette, add the **sensor value** block to the first position of the **greater than** block, and select the **slider** option. Enter the number **20** in the second value of the **greater than** block.

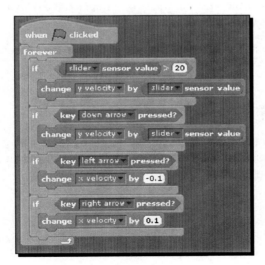

7. Give it a go. Click the flag and move the slider. Enable the slider sensor watcher to display the slider value on the stage.

As long as the slider's value is greater than 20, the marble rises. We can still use the right and left arrow keys to move the marbles across the stage.

What just happened?

This was another example where we substituted a keyboard input with a sensor value from the PicoBoard. This time we used a sprite that was configured to demonstrate gravity. As the slider measured a value of 20, the marble rose. When we reduced the slider value to less than 20, the marble dropped.

If we examine the gravity marble scripts, we learn that the marble will always fall unless it's acted on by some other force. In this case, the force that moves the marble up is the slider. Let the slider value fall below 20, and the marble falls -0.05 pixels at a time.

Using gravity

Stand up from your chair and jump up as high as you can. Grab a pencil and toss it to the ceiling. You know this story. Gravity grounds everything in real life.

When we design games with jumping sprites or falling objects, we can make the game more realistic by adding gravity. And it doesn't matter if we use a PicoBoard, an arrow key, or some other input.

Have a go hero

Want to accelerate the marble's rise up the stage? Replace the 0.1 value in the **change y velocity** block to use the slider sensor value.

Watch the marble take off. Try adjusting the rate of the marble's ascent in other ways using the slider sensor value.

Create circuits

We could teach our kids about electrical current by giving them a plug and an outlet, but that seems dangerous. Instead, we'll use Scratch, a PicoBoard, and an alligator clip to demonstrate electrical resistance.

Time for action – complete the circuit

Once again, we will find a sprite that has some scripts attached to it and modify the control to work with the alligator clips on the PicoBoard:

1. Start a new Scratch project and select **choose new sprite from file**.

2. Delete the original sprite.

3. Open the **Fantasy** folder and select the **Jumping Jack** sprite.

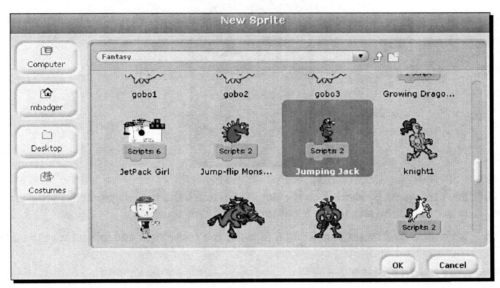

4. Replace the **key up arrow pressed?** block with the **sensor** block and select the **A connected** option.

5. Replace the **key right arrow pressed?** block with the **sensor** block and select the **B connected** option.

6. Replace the **key left arrow pressed?** block with the **sensor** block and select the **C connected** option.

7. The PicoBoard has four connectors labeled A, B, C, and D. Plug a set of alligator clips into each of the A, B, and C sensors.

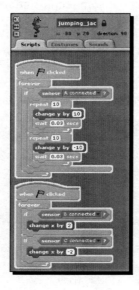

8. Start the game by clicking on the flag. Then, touch the two alligator clips attached to sensor A. The jack jumps for as long as the clips touch.

9. Touch the clips on sensors B and C to move the sprite right and left across the stage.

What just happened?

When we touched the ends of the alligator clip, we completed a circuit and our sprite reacted by jumping or moving across the stage. Like the button, these sensors reported a true or false value. When the clips at the end of one of the wires were touched, the value was true.

Wiring our projects

When we touch the alligator clips together, we basically replicate a switch, like the one that turns the light on and off in our room. When we turn on a switch, we complete a circuit.

If we had a real switch, we could connect a clip to each connector and then use the switch to toggle the project on and off.

 You can only create a circuit using the alligator clips attached to a single sensor. In other words, connecting the clips on sensor A to sensor B will not create a circuit, and the values for sensors A and B will remain false.

The alligator clips also measure the electrical resistance of the circuit on a scale of 0 to 100. We can use any material capable of carrying an electrical current to connect the alligator clips. Example materials might be foil, fingernail clippers, or other metals.

Measure electrical resistance

Before you start this exercise, collect a piece of foil, a wet napkin, and a wooden pencil. Feel free to substitute using your creativity.

Time for action – measure resistance

We'll continue to modify our **Jumping Jack** sprite that's configured to work with sensors A, B, and C:

1. Plug the fourth alligator clip into sensor D on the PicoBoard.

2. In the Scratch project, add a **forever** block to the second script of the **Jumping Jack** sprite.

3. From the **Sound** palette, add the **play note** block to the **forever** block.

4. We'll use the resistance value to select the note to play. From the **Sensing** palette, add the **sensor value** block to the **play note** block. Select **sensor D** from the list of options.

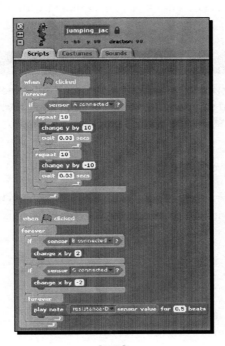

5. Click the flag, and let's test some resistance. In turn, attach the foil, the wet napkin, and the pencil to the alligator clips attached to sensor D.

6. If you want to watch the resistance values, enable the sensor value monitor for sensor D.

What just happened?

Feels like science class, doesn't it? Not surprisingly, our test materials showed various levels of resistance, and as we connected the alligator clips to each material, a different note played.

Actually, the tinfoil didn't play a note, and if you watched the sensor values, you noted that sensor D reported zero when we connected the foil. This means that the current flowed through without resistance. At the other extreme was our pencil; it reported a resistance value of 100, and the music played steadily.

Using resistance

We know that current flows through foil easily, but not wood. Our tests confirm that water conducts a current, but not as well as foil, for example. When we measure electrical resistance, we want to know by how much the material impedes an electrical current. In the case of our PicoBoard sensor, the higher the value, the more the material impedes the current. How we use that value is left to our imagination.

Using the PicoBoard sensors allows our kids to experiment with the electrical properties of various materials.

Have a go hero

Continue measuring the resistance of various materials. Find some material and connect it to your sensor to measure and compare the values of each item. If you'd like, you can also use the resistance value to transform the sprite's graphical properties.

Watch all sensor values

As we've seen throughout our projects, it can be helpful to watch the values associated with the PicoBoard sensors. In addition to selectively watching the sensor values, we can watch them all at one time.

From the **Sensing** palette, right-click on the **sensor** block and select the **show ScratchBoard watcher** option.

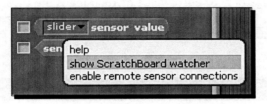

ScratchBoard was the predecessor to the PicoBoard. Selecting the ScratchBoard watcher places a monitor on the stage that shows all the sensors. Refer to the following screenshot:

As you look at the screenshot, you might think that some of the values are missing. The alligator clip sensors measure resistance, as the picture shows. However, the alligator clip sensors also report a true or false value to indicate when the clips touch. Why doesn't the ScratchBoard watcher show the Boolean value of the alligator clip sensors?

Have I led you enough yet? As you might guess, the Boolean values of the alligator clips are reported. We just have to interpret the true and false. In the screenshot, sensors A, B, and C report 100 while sensor D reports zero.

We know from our experiments that a value of 100 means no current is flowing. The alligator clips might as well be disconnected, and the answer to the question, "Is sensor A connected?" would be false. By contrast, a sensor value of zero indicates the current is flowing freely and that the clips are connected.

Have a go hero

So, we know that an alligator clip sensor value of 100 means the clips aren't connected, and a value of zero means the clips are connected. What if the resistance is somewhere in between? Are the alligator clips connected? Attach the alligator clips for sensor A to the wet napkin to find out.

Pop quiz

1. PicoBoards cannot be used with projects that are shared on the Web.

   ◆ True

   ◆ False

2. Which of the following PicoBoard sensors are measured with numeric values?

   ◆ Sound

   ◆ Light

   ◆ Alligator clips

   ◆ All of the above

3. If you want to view all the sensor values on the screen at one time, you:

   ◆ Right-click on the **sensor** block and choose **enable remote sensor connections**.

   ◆ Right-click on the **sensor** block and choose **show ScratchBoard watcher**.

   ◆ You can't view all sensor values at one time

LEGO WeDo support

Starting with version 1.4, Scratch can connect to the LEGO Eduction WeDo robotics kits with motor blocks. And even though I'm not showing examples in this book, it's a feature worth mentioning.

To show the LEGO WeDo blocks, select the **Show motor blocks** from the **Edit** menu.

Summary

We saw how easy it was to connect Scratch to a webcam, and then import those images into our projects. We then exported the images from our webcam as a new sprite for use in other projects.

As we have seen, the PicoBoard easily integrates real-world stimuli into our Scratch projects. All the previous programming concepts we learned still apply when we connect the PicoBoard. The board enables interactivity in many creative ways:

- We used our own voice to transform a sprite and change the background.
- We used our slideshow to display the next slide by pressing the PicoBoard's button.
- By increasing the light, we made our **dragon** sprite shoot a bigger flame.
- We demonstrated gravity with the slider sensor.
- Using the alligator clips, we made our **Jumping Jack** sprite sing and dance based on the amount of electrical resistance.

That's it. You're ready to show the world your Scratch programming skills. You have all the tools you need to turn your imagination into your very own mad scientist's laboratory.

Scratch Resources

Where do you turn when you need inspiration, sprites, images, sounds, and other information? When you need inspiration, sprites, images, sounds, and additional information, use the following list of select Scratch resources:

Resource	Web Address	What You'll Find
Scratch Guide	www.scratchguide.com	◆ Workshops ◆ Related book content
Wikipedia	www.wikipedia.org	◆ Content ◆ Images ◆ Inspiration
The Spriters Resource	www.spriters-resource.com	◆ Sprites
Learn Scratch	www.learnscratch.org	◆ Lesson plans
Scratch Resources	resources.scratchr.org	◆ Sprites ◆ Sounds
Scratch Forums	Scratch.mit.edu/forums	◆ Community support
Freeloops.com	www.freeloops.com	◆ Music loops
Educator Resources	info.scratch.mit.edu/Educators	◆ Research papers ◆ Videos ◆ Documentation

Resource	Web Address	What You'll Find
Creative Commons	www.creativecommons.org	◆ Images ◆ Sounds
Flickr	www.flickr.com	◆ Images (search for creative commons)
The Freesound Project	www.freesound.org	◆ Sound effects
Scratch Project Site	Scratch.mit.edu	◆ Everything Scratch

Index

Packt Open Source Project Royalties

When we sell a book written on an Open Source project, we pay a royalty directly to that project. Therefore by purchasing Scratch 1.4: *Beginner's Guide*, Packt will have given some of the money received to the Scratch project.

In the long term, we see ourselves and you—customers and readers of our books—as part of the Open Source ecosystem, providing sustainable revenue for the projects we publish on. Our aim at Packt is to establish publishing royalties as an essential part of the service and support a business model that sustains Open Source.

If you're working with an Open Source project that you would like us to publish on, and subsequently pay royalties to, please get in touch with us.

Writing for Packt

We welcome all inquiries from people who are interested in authoring. Book proposals should be sent to author@packtpub.com. If your book idea is still at an early stage and you would like to discuss it first before writing a formal book proposal, contact us; one of our commissioning editors will get in touch with you.

We're not just looking for published authors; if you have strong technical skills but no writing experience, our experienced editors can help you develop a writing career, or simply get some additional reward for your expertise.

About Packt Publishing

Packt, pronounced 'packed', published its first book "Mastering phpMyAdmin for Effective MySQL Management" in April 2004 and subsequently continued to specialize in publishing highly focused books on specific technologies and solutions.

Our books and publications share the experiences of your fellow IT professionals in adapting and customizing today's systems, applications, and frameworks. Our solution-based books give you the knowledge and power to customize the software and technologies you're using to get the job done. Packt books are more specific and less general than the IT books you have seen in the past. Our unique business model allows us to bring you more focused information, giving you more of what you need to know, and less of what you don't.

Packt is a modern, yet unique publishing company, which focuses on producing quality, cutting-edge books for communities of developers, administrators, and newbies alike. For more information, please visit our website: www.PacktPub.com.

Moodle 1.9 for Teaching 7-14 Year Olds
Beginner's Guide

ISBN: 978-1-847197-14-6   Paperback: 236 pages

Effective e-learning for younger students using Moodle as your Classroom Assistant

1. Focus on the unique needs of young learners to create a fun, interesting, interactive, and informative learning environment your students will want to go on day after day

2. Engage and motivate your students with games, quizzes, movies, and podcasts the whole class can participate in

3. Go paperless! Put your lessons online and grade them anywhere, anytime

Moodle Course Conversion
Beginner's Guide

ISBN: 978-1-847195-24-1   Paperback: 316 pages

Taking existing classes online quickly with the Moodle LMS

1. No need to start from scratch! This book shows you the quickest way to start using Moodle and e-learning, by bringing your existing lesson materials into Moodle

2. Move your existing course notes, worksheets, and resources into Moodle quickly then improve your course, taking advantage of multimedia and collaboration

3. Moving marking online – no more backbreaking boxes of assignments to lug to and from school or colleges

Please check **www.PacktPub.com** for information on our titles